House Beautiful
Food for Friends

House Beautiful
Food for Friends

Over 180 recipes for easy entertaining

CAROLINE ATKINS

CASSELL

Caroline Atkins and *House Beautiful* magazine would like to thank the
following people for their contributions to this book:

Recipes: Jane Mather and Berit Vinegrad
Photographs: Debbie Patterson, Spike Powell and Lucinda Symons
Co-ordination: Lucy Allnutt, Libby Norman and Gill Rothwell

Cassell
Wellington House
125 Strand
London WC2R 0BB
www.cassell.co.uk

Distributed in the United States by
Sterling Publishing Co., Inc.
387 Park Avenue South
New York, NY 10016–8810

British Library Cataloguing-in-Publication Data

A catalogue record for this book is available
from the British Library

ISBN 0-304-35166-0

Edited by Wendy Hobson
Designed by Richard Carr

Printed and bound in China by Colorcraft Ltd.

Contents

Introduction

THERE'S A real sense of satisfaction in putting together a meal that perfectly suits the occasion, the season and the people who are going to eat it. *Food for Friends* is the ideal entertainer's companion because it is designed as a series of menus tailor-made for different occasions throughout the year – although they can all be mixed and matched in an infinite number of ways to suit any event at any time.

We can all remember favourite meals that have left an impression on us – holiday memories, childhood picnic treats, the sheer pleasure of eating out of doors in summer or of shutting out the cold with a warming winter feast. These recipes recapture that spirit. And because the real pleasure of good food is enjoying it with friends, we've added time-saving tips where possible and included ready-prepared ingredients in many recipes.

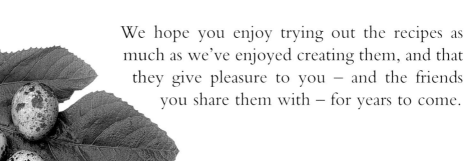

We hope you enjoy trying out the recipes as much as we've enjoyed creating them, and that they give pleasure to you – and the friends you share them with – for years to come.

A Taste of

Summer

WITH ITS longer days and relaxed pace, summer is an ideal time to catch up on your entertaining. So don't feel guilty about all those invitations you owe; it's easy to serve up a spread that everyone will enjoy. The best menus combine the freshest flavours of the season with sunshine colours and an unmistakable sense of holiday.

Quick and Easy Dinner Party

T HE STUNNING *elegance of this summer feast disguises its simplicity. Entertaining friends should be a treat, not a test, so we devised a menu that everyone can excel at, leaving you plenty of time to relax and enjoy the evening.*

Menu for eight

BRUSCHETTAS WITH
ASPARAGUS AND PEPPERS
—
ROAST SEA BASS
—
CHEAT'S PEACH FLAN
—
CHEESEBOARD

Instead of a formal first course, try serving a selection of canapés: roasted strips of yellow pepper, stir-fried asparagus spears and bruschettas with a choice of toppings.

Bruschettas with asparagus and peppers

Crisp-baked baguette and two delicious toppings make this simple Italian-style starter.

SERVES 8

4 large yellow peppers
120 ml (4 fl oz) olive oil
24–32 large asparagus
    spears, trimmed
16 baguette slices, cut on
    the diagonal
4–5 tsp black olive paste
250 g (9 oz) Mozzarella
    cheese, sliced
salt and freshly ground
    black pepper
a few basil leaves, shredded
200–225 g (7–8 oz) goats'
    cheese
1 eating apple, sliced

TO SERVE

mayonnaise
crème fraîche
    or natural yoghurt

1 Preheat the oven to 230°C/450°F/gas mark 8.

2 Place the peppers on a baking tray, drizzle with oil and roast in the oven for about 20 minutes until the skin is slightly charred. Place in a plastic bag and leave to cool.

3 Peel off and discard the skins and seeds. Slice the flesh into long strips.

4 Meanwhile, heat a little of the oil in a frying pan. Toss in the asparagus spears and cook for 2–3 minutes over a fairly high heat until they are just tender but still crisp. Set aside.

5 To make the olive and Mozzarella bruschettas, reduce the oven temperature to 220°C/425°F/gas mark 7. Brush eight baguette slices on both sides with olive oil and bake in the oven for 10 minutes. Spread the olive paste over one side and top with Mozzarella. Season and garnish with torn basil leaves just before serving.

6 To make the goats' cheese bruschettas, preheat the grill to medium-hot and toast the remaining baguette slices on one side only. Brush the untoasted side of the bread with olive oil, then top with the goats' cheese and slices of apple. Grill until the cheese starts to bubble.

7 Arrange the asparagus, peppers and bruschettas on a large serving plate and serve with a bowl of mayonnaise blended with a little crème fraîche or natural yoghurt to taste.

Roast sea bass

This dish is simple to make and impressively different, providing a delicious alternative to classic salmon.

SERVES 8

1.75 kg (4 lb) sea bass, scaled and gutted
salt and freshly ground black pepper

3–4 tbsp chopped fresh flatleaf parsley
3 tbsp chopped sweet fennel
1 tbsp chopped fresh marjoram
2 garlic cloves, chopped
juice of $\frac{1}{2}$ lemon
4 tbsp olive oil
1 lemon, cut into wedges

FOR THE SAUCE

50 g (2 oz) butter
50 g (2 oz) plain flour
600 ml (1 pint) milk
1 tbsp freshly grated horseradish

TO SERVE

steamed runner beans
boiled new potatoes

1 Preheat the oven to 200°C/400°F/gas mark 6.

2 Wipe the fish inside and out with kitchen paper and season with plenty of salt and pepper.

3 Mix the parsley, fennel, marjoram and garlic. Fill the inside of the fish with the herb mixture and place on a roasting tray.

4 Pour the lemon juice over the fish, then drizzle generously with olive oil. Roast in the oven for 30–35 minutes until the flesh flakes easily when tested with a fork.

5 While the fish is cooking, make a basic white sauce. Melt the butter, then stir in the flour to make a firm paste. Cook gently for 1 minute, stirring continuously, then remove from the heat and gradually stir in the milk. Return to the heat and gradually bring to the boil, stirring all the time until the sauce thickens. Simmer gently for 3 minutes, remove from the heat, season and stir in a little freshly grated horseradish to taste.

6 Serve the fish on a bed of steamed runner beans and garnished with lemon wedges, with some boiled new potatoes and the horseradish sauce.

Sea bass is in season from May to September. If your local fishmonger doesn't have it, ask them to recommend a similar fish.

Cheat's peach flan

To make this look even prettier, you can place almonds in the hollows of the peach halves. If you prefer fresh peaches, halve and stone 8–10 and poach them in 600 ml (1 pint) of water and 300 g (10 oz) of caster sugar for about 10 minutes or until just tender.

SERVES 8

- 3 x 400 g (14 oz) tins of peach halves, drained
- 25 cm (10 in) pastry flan case
- 2 large eggs
- 25 g (1 oz) caster sugar
- 75 g (3 oz) butter, melted
- 120 ml (4 fl oz) Greek yoghurt
- 175 ml (6 fl oz) single cream
- 50 g (2 oz) flaked almonds

1 Preheat the oven to 220°C/425°F/gas mark 7.

2 Arrange the peaches in the flan case. Beat together the eggs, caster sugar, melted butter, yoghurt and cream. Pour over the fruit and bake in the oven for 20 minutes, then reduce the heat to 180°C/350°F/gas mark 4 and bake for a further 10–15 minutes until the custard is firm and golden brown. Sprinkle with almonds and serve cold or at room temperature.

For the perfect end to a summer meal, serve a selection of cheeses with fresh fruit such as grapes or physalis and a glass of white port.

Opposite: *Our cheat's peach flan cuts corners on preparation time without sacrificing any of the taste. Store-cupboard ingredients like tinned peaches and a ready-made flan case are transformed with a rich custard to make a mouthwatering dessert.*

Cheeseboard

When you make a cheeseboard selection, don't try to serve too many varieties; a well-balanced selection of a few different cheeses is better than a wide range. Make sure they are all in perfect condition and at room temperature before you serve, and leave the rind on for guests to trim away if they wish. Select a contrast in texture, colour and flavour: one hard cheese, one blue cheese and one or two ripe, soft cheeses makes a good combination.

Serve your cheeseboard with a selection of crisp savoury biscuits or crackers and garnish with fruit such as physalis or grapes.

SETTING THE SCENE

Whether you are serving your meal inside or out, opt for a simple table setting and decorate the table with flowers to complement your crockery and table linen.

Tropical Paradise

S PICY AND CITRUS, this is the menu to conjure up a carnival mood. Most of the ingredients are available from supermarkets, and we've used ready-prepared sauces and seasonings to keep things easy. It's an instant trip to the tropics and irresistibly tasty.

Menu for four

SPICY SALT COD AND SWEETCORN FRITTERS

—

COCONUT CHICKEN WITH LIME PAPAYA

OKRA AND CALLALOO

FRIED PLANTAIN RICE WITH BEANS

—

SPICE ISLANDS PIE

HONEY AND NUTMEG ICE CREAM

—

CLASSIC PIÑA COLADA

TROPICAL RUM PUNCH

SETTING THE SCENE

Bright colours are perfect for this tropical menu and you can really go to town with your table setting to create an exotic holiday mood. We used blues, yellows and limes to complement the vivid tropical ingredients in our menu. For an authentic finishing touch, use place mats made of banana leaves – they're widely available in ethnic grocery stores and markets.

Spicy salt cod and sweetcorn fritters

Salt cod is available from delicatessens, fishmongers and markets. If you can't find it locally, or don't have time for overnight soaking, tinned crab meat makes a tasty alternative.

SERVES 4

175 g (6 oz) salt cod
100 g (4 oz) plain flour
$\frac{1}{2}$ tsp baking powder
salt
100 ml (3$\frac{1}{2}$ fl oz) water
100 g (4 oz) tin of sweetcorn
2 spring onions, chopped
2 tsp wood jerk seasoning
olive oil

TO SERVE

**green salad or tropical fruit
hot pepper sauce**

1 Soak the salt cod overnight in cold water. Next day rinse well, remove all the bones and skin and flake the flesh into small pieces.

2 Mix together the flour, baking powder and salt with enough of the water to form a batter. Add all the other ingredients to the batter and stir very gently.

3 Heat a little oil and shallow-fry spoonfuls of the batter mixture over a medium heat for 1–2 minutes until golden, turning once. Gently remove from the pan and drain on kitchen paper. Serve hot with green salad or tropical fruit and hot pepper sauce.

Coconut chicken with lime papaya

Far Eastern flavours are always popular and add a subtle fragrance to the menu. Oriental ingredients are easy to find in major stores.

SERVES 4

4 skinless chicken breasts
4 tsp hot pepper sauce
1 garlic clove, crushed
sea salt
4 spring onions, thinly sliced lengthways
300 ml (10 fl oz) coconut cream
1 large, firm but ripe papaya, peeled and seeded
juice of 1 lime
snipped fresh chives

1 Preheat the oven to 180°C/350°F/gas mark 4.

2 Score the underside of the chicken four times with a sharp knife, rub with hot pepper sauce, crushed garlic and sea salt and lay seasoned-side down in an ovenproof dish. Chop three of the sliced spring onions and sprinkle over the chicken.

3 Pour the coconut cream around the chicken, place a quarter of papaya alongside each breast, then cover with foil and cook in the oven for 20–25 minutes or until the chicken is no longer pink and feels tender when you insert a knife.

4 Squeeze the lime juice over the chicken, spoon a little sauce on to each plate, place the chicken and papaya on top and scatter with chives and the remaining spring onion.

Okra and callaloo

If you can't buy callaloo, use spinach or Chinese leaves instead. For a less spicy version of the dish, reduce the amount of scotch bonnet chilli pepper or leave it out altogether.

SERVES 4

1 tbsp olive oil
300 g (11 oz) okra
1 tsp chopped scotch bonnet chilli pepper
500 g (18 oz) tin of callaloo, drained
salt and freshly ground black pepper

1 Heat the oil and fry the okra and chilli pepper for 3–4 minutes.

2 Add the callaloo to the okra and chilli pepper and cook until heated through. Season with salt and pepper and serve immediately.

Chicken breasts with coconut and fresh papaya are easy to prepare and taste delicious served with okra and callaloo.

Fried plantain rice with beans

This is particularly good served with green plantain chips: cut plantain into fingers, shallow-fry and serve sprinkled with salt, hot pepper sauce and chopped fresh parsley or coriander. Remember that the oil from chilli peppers can irritate delicate skin (particularly your lips and around your eyes) so rub your hands lightly with olive oil before preparing them and wash your hands and utensils thoroughly afterwards. If you don't have rice already cooked, you'll need about 50 g (2 oz) uncooked weight.

SERVES 4

2 yellow plantains, peeled and chopped

2 tbsp olive oil

1 onion, chopped

$\frac{1}{4}$ yellow scotch bonnet chilli pepper, chopped

225 g (8 oz) cooked white rice

100 g (4 oz) cooked or tinned kidney beans, drained

2 tbsp chopped fresh parsley

salt and freshly ground black pepper

1 To peel plantain, cut off each end and make three length-long slits with a sharp knife. Then, using your fingers, peel away the tough skin.

2 Heat half the oil and fry the onion and chilli pepper until soft, then remove from the pan and set aside.

3 Add the remaining oil to the pan, then fry the plantain for about 5 minutes until just turning golden.

4 Return the fried onion and pepper to the pan and add the rice and kidney beans. Stir until heated through. Add the parsley and seasoning and serve.

Spice Islands pie

Sweet potato is a classic Caribbean main-course vegetable, but its rich, sweet taste works equally well in this creamy pie.

SERVES 4

1 large sweet potato, cooked

50 g (2 oz) sultanas

juice and grated zest of 1 orange

1 tsp ground ginger

2 eggs

300 ml (10 fl oz) double cream

1 x 25–30 cm (10–12 in) pastry case, baked

1 Preheat the oven to 180°C/350°F/gas mark 4.

2 Mash the sweet potato, then stir in the sultanas, orange juice and zest and ginger.

3 In a separate bowl, lightly beat the eggs and cream, then fold this into the sweet potato mixture.

4 Spoon the mixture into the pastry case and cook in the centre of the oven for 20–30 minutes. The centre should remain soft. Leave to stand for 15 minutes before cutting and serving.

Honey and nutmeg ice cream

This is delicious on its own so if you don't have time to make the pie, just serve the ice cream with a tropical fruit salad of star fruit and mango with a squeeze of fresh lime and Angostura bitters. And if you're really short of time, serve a good-quality vanilla ice cream sprinkled with freshly grated nutmeg.

SERVES 4

2 egg whites

50 g (2 oz) icing sugar, sifted

2 tbsp clear honey

150 ml (5 fl oz) double cream

150 ml (5 fl oz) ready-made custard

$1\frac{1}{2}$ tsp grated nutmeg

1 Whisk the egg whites until stiff. Gradually add the sugar and honey and continue to whisk for 5 minutes.

2 Lightly whip the cream, then fold into the egg white with the custard and nutmeg.

3 Turn out into a freezer container and freeze for 8 hours or overnight. Allow to soften slightly in the fridge before serving.

Classic piña colada

An ideal drink to get the carnival spirit going.

SERVES 4

750 ml (1¼ pints) pineapple juice
200 ml (7 fl oz) coconut cream
250 ml (8 fl oz) white rum
juice of 1 lime
crushed ice

Combine all the ingredients in a liquidizer or cocktail shaker. Serve immediately with a tropical fruit skewer.

Tropical rum punch

If you make a fruit salad, reserve some of the fruit from your fruit salad to make a garnish for this Caribbean-style punch.

SERVES 4

1 litre (1¾ pints) tropical fruit juice
250 ml (8 fl oz) dark rum
juice of 1 lime
crushed ice

Make sure the fruit juice is well chilled. Combine all the ingredients and serve with a skewer laden with tropical fruit. Serve immediately.

FINISHING TOUCHES

With such a robust and spicy meal, you can afford to pick really dramatic flowers in hot reds and lime greens. It's easy to supplement the colour with chrysanthemums, lilies and bright foliage from the garden, and don't forget to add a bowl of citrus fruit to your table setting to complete the tropical effect.

Mediterranean Buffet

F OR ANYONE *suffering guilt pangs about return invitations owed to friends, the ideal menu is a buffet that can be adapted to suit the number of guests and that requires little or no cooking on the day. We've chosen dishes that are suitable for serving indoors or out – including a super-cool ice bowl centrepiece that's guaranteed to impress.*

Menu for twenty

ITALIAN ANTIPASTO

HERB AND TOMATO BREAD

—

MEDITERRANEAN PORK AND ROASTED PEPPER CASSEROLE

PERFECT PARTY RICE

MIXED-LEAF SALAD

—

MELON ICE BOWL

CHOCOLATE MADELEINES WITH RASPBERRY COULIS

Italian antipasto

SERVES 20

Buy an assortment of meats – slices of bresaola, prosciutto, pastrami and several types of salami – allowing 40–50 g (1½ –2 oz) per person. Arrange on a large plate garnished with basil and serve with chilli pickles, marinated mushrooms and marinated Feta cheese.

Chilli pickles

SERVES 20

2 x 250 g (9 oz) jars of pickled cocktail gherkins
150 ml (5 fl oz) cider vinegar
100 ml (3½ fl oz) water
50 g (2 oz) caster sugar
a pinch of crushed dried red chilli peppers

1 Drain the gherkins and place them in a glass or ceramic jar.

2 Mix the remaining ingredients and pour over the gherkins. Cover and leave to marinate overnight or longer.

Marinated mushrooms

SERVES 20

2 x 275 g (10 oz) jars
  of sliced antipasto
  mushrooms
juice of 1 orange
juice and grated zest of
  1 lemon
1 garlic clove, crushed
1 tbsp crushed coriander
  seeds
2 tsp soy sauce
1 tbsp chopped fresh
  coriander

1 Drain the mushrooms and put them in one large or several smaller serving dishes.

2 Blend the remaining ingredients and pour the dressing over the mushrooms. Leave to marinate for 2–3 hours.

Marinated Feta cheese

SERVES 20

700 g (1½ lb) Feta cheese
250 ml (9 fl oz) extra virgin
  olive oil
2 tsp paprika
1 tbsp fresh thyme
freshly ground black pepper
50 g (2 oz) pine nuts

1 Cut the cheese into 2 cm (¾ in) cubes and place in a bowl.

2 Blend the oil, paprika and thyme and grind over some pepper. Pour over the cheese and toss gently.

3 Toast the pine nuts in a hot frying pan, shaking continuously until the nuts are speckled brown. Cool on a plate then toss into the Feta. Marinate until required.

Herb and tomato bread

This delicious loaf is very easy to make, although if you are really short of time, you could take advantage of the range of interesting Italian breads in the supermarket. Many are part-baked so you can still achieve a freshly baked flavour.

MAKES 3 LOAVES

1.5 kg (3 lb) plain flour
a pinch of salt
2 sachets of fast-action dried yeast
250 ml (8 fl oz) extra virgin olive oil
200 ml (7 fl oz) dry white wine
550 ml (18 fl oz) lukewarm water

FOR THE TOPPING

sage leaves, cut into strips, or rosemary leaves
sun-dried tomatoes, cut into slivers
crystal or flake sea salt
olive oil

1 Mix the flour, salt and yeast in a large bowl. Add the oil, wine and water and mix to a dough. Knead on a lightly floured surface until smooth and no longer sticky.

2 Oil the dough lightly, then return it to the bowl. Cover with clingfilm and leave for 1½ hours until the dough has doubled in size.

3 Preheat the oven to 230°C/450°F/gas mark 8.

4 Knead the dough briefly on a floured surface, then divide into three equal pieces. Roll into 2 cm (¾ in) thick round or oval loaves.

5 Place the loaves on oiled baking sheets and make indentations over the surface with your fingertips. Scatter with strips of sage leaves or rosemary leaves and slivers of sun-dried tomatoes, then sprinkle with a little sea salt.

6 Bake in the oven for 25 minutes or until golden brown and baked through. Brush with olive oil and serve.

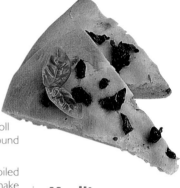

Mediterranean pork and roasted pepper casserole

This rich, tasty dish is delicious served with a fresh mixed-leaf salad. Make a selection of the different salad leaves now available in greengrocers and supermarkets.

SERVES 20

3.5 kg (8 lb) boneless leg of pork, trimmed of fat
8 red peppers
8 yellow or orange peppers
150 ml (5 fl oz) olive oil
2 red onions, chopped
3 garlic cloves, crushed
3 tbsp plain flour
225 g (8 oz) stoned kalamata olives
a few thyme sprigs
a pinch of crushed dried red chilli peppers (optional)
salt and freshly ground black pepper
2 tbsp chopped fresh parsley

FOR THE MARINADE

1 litre (1¾ pints) red wine
85 ml (3 fl oz) balsamic vinegar
120 ml (4 fl oz) olive oil
2 red onions, roughly chopped
3 bay leaves, torn into pieces
8–10 thyme sprigs
1 heaped tbsp allspice berries, lightly crushed
pared zest of 1 lemon

1 Cut the meat into 2.5 cm (1 in) cubes and place in a large bowl. Add the marinade ingredients and toss well. Cover and leave to marinate in the fridge for 24–36 hours, turning occasionally.

2 Preheat the oven to 230°C/450°F/gas mark 8.

3 Place the peppers on a baking tray, drizzle with a little of the oil and roast in the oven for about 20 minutes until the skin is wrinkled and slightly charred. Place in a plastic bag and leave to cool.

4 Peel off and discard the skins and seeds. Slice the flesh into strips. Chill in a covered bowl until required.

5 Drain the meat. Strain and reserve the marinade. Heat a little oil in a large flame-proof casserole dish. Brown the meat in batches until golden, removing it with a slot-ted spoon and adding more oil to the dish as required. Fry the onions and garlic until lightly browned, then stir in the flour. Return the meat to the dish with the olives, thyme, chillies and seasoning.

6 In a separate pan, bring the marinade to the boil, then boil rapidly for 2 minutes. Pour through a fine strainer into the casserole dish and stir.

Perfect party rice and a mixed salad make a great accompaniment to our Mediterranean pork and roasted pepper casserole

7 Reduce the oven tem-perature to 160°C/325°F/ gas mark 3 and cook the casserole for 1½ hours. Add the peppers, then return to the oven for a further 1 hour. Stir in the parsley, season to taste and serve.

Perfect party rice

This can be served either hot with a main course, or cold as a salad-style accompaniment. The fresh herbs give it a wonderful flavour.

SERVES 20

1 kg (2¼ lb) American long-grain easy-cook rice
salt
75–100 g (3–4 oz) salted butter
1 large garlic clove, crushed
grated zest of 1 lemon
a pinch of grated nutmeg
2 tbsp snipped fresh chives
2 tbsp chopped fresh coriander
2 tbsp chopped fresh parsley
450 g (1 lb) frozen peas

1 Plunge the rice into a large pan of lightly salted, boiling water. Return to the boil, then simmer for 15 minutes. Drain well.

2 Meanwhile, melt the butter over a gentle heat. Stir in the garlic, lemon zest, nutmeg and herbs. Remove from the heat.

3 Plunge the peas into a pan of lightly salted, boiling water. Return to the boil, then drain.

4 Place the herb butter and peas in a warmed serving dish. Add the rice and toss together well.

Melon ice bowl

Ice bowls create a wonderful centrepiece. You need two plastic or metal bowls of similar shape, one fitting snugly inside the other. The outer bowl should have a 3.5–4 litre (6–7 pint) capacity, the inner bowl a 2.5–2.75 litre (4½–5 pint) capacity. Vary the type and quantity of melons to suit the occasion.

SERVES 20

mint leaves or flower petals
1 ripe ogen or galia melon
1 charentais melon
1 honeydew melon
1 small water melon

1 Fill the larger bowl about half full with water and place the inner bowl inside. Weigh down inner bowl by placing weights inside it. Add or remove water until it is a little below the top of the outer bowl. Float mint leaves or flower petals in the water to decorate.

2 Secure by fixing strong tape from the inside of the inner bowl across to the outside of the outer bowl. Freeze overnight.

3 Remove from the freezer and run cold water around the bowls to loosen them from the ice. Place the

Chocolate madeleines with raspberry coulis

Shell-shaped madeleine moulds are available from kitchen shops. They are quite shallow so the cooking time is short; if you use different-sized cake moulds, you may need to adjust the time.

MAKES 20

FOR THE MADELEINES

175 g (6 oz) butter, at room temperature

175 g (6 oz) caster sugar

3 eggs

1 tsp almond essence

90 g (3½ oz) plain flour

3 tbsp cocoa powder

1 tsp baking powder

100 g (4 oz) ground almonds

icing sugar, sifted

FOR THE COULIS

900 g (2 lb) fresh or thawed raspberries

150 ml (5 fl oz) Kirsch or cassis liqueur

sugar to taste

1 Preheat the oven to 190°C/375°F/gas mark 5.

2 To make the madeleines, beat together the butter, sugar and eggs until light and fluffy. Beat in the almond essence and 2 tbsp of flour.

3 Sift together the remaining flour, the cocoa and baking powder. Fold into the egg mixture, then fold in the ground almonds.

4 Fill 20 well-greased madeleine moulds two-thirds full and bake in the oven for 15 minutes until golden brown and firm.

5 Turn out of the moulds and leave to cool on a rack. When cold, store in an airtight container. Just before serving, dust with sifted icing sugar.

6 To make the coulis, liquidize the berries with the liqueur.

7 Push through a nylon sieve to remove the seeds.

8 Sweeten to taste. Chill until shortly before serving with the sugar-dusted madeleines.

Above: *Leave the ice bowl in the freezer until the last minute and it will stay frozen for the whole evening. Dust the chocolate madeleines with sifted icing sugar before serving.*

ice bowl on a serving plate and keep in the freezer until ready to serve the melon salad.

4 For the salad, peel and seed the melons, then cut the flesh into cubes. Toss together and chill before serving in the ice bowl.

Sun-drenched Supper

This MENU *was designed to capture the colours and flavours of late summer. Crisp salads, fresh salmon and a choice of two wonderfully indulgent desserts are the perfect combination of classic ingredients that make the best use of the season's produce.*

Sweet melons with Feta cheese

You can easily vary the quantities of this simple starter depending on the number of your guests; you need about half a melon and 50 g (2 oz) of Feta per person. Use a mixture of melons for the best flavour and colour.

SERVES 6

1 galia melon
1 cantaloupe melon
1 honeydew melon
a few chervil sprigs
olive oil
freshly ground white pepper
300 g (11 oz) Feta cheese

1 Peel and seed the melons, then cut the flesh into small slices and place in a large bowl with a scattering of chervil sprigs, a drizzle of olive oil and a little white pepper. Leave to stand at room temperature for 10 minutes.

2 Place the melon on individual plates and crumble the Feta on top.

SETTING THE SCENE
Delicious summer colours set off the rich golden tones of our celebration menu. Look for china in soft shades of green, blue, turquoise and custard yellow, and add extra colour with your table linen. You can really go to town with gold-coloured napkin rings, shiny foil-wrapped sweets and even little brass finger bowls. Burnt orange lilies make a fabulous finishing touch, adding exotic colour and a heady summer scent.

Baked salmon with fried lemon slices

A 2 kg (4¼ lb) fish is enough for six people. For ten guests, select a 3 kg (7 lb) fish and increase the quantities of the other ingredients in proportion. If you are cooking a larger fish, add a further 10 minutes per 500 g (18 oz). Unless you have a large oven, you might find it easier to cook two smaller fish rather than one large one.

SERVES 6

1 x 2 kg (4½ lb) salmon
½ tsp fennel seeds
salt and freshly ground
    white pepper
1 tbsp olive oil
2 lemons, sliced
6 cherry tomatoes
flatleaf parsley sprigs

1 Preheat the oven to 150°C/300°F/gas mark 2. Lay a sheet of foil on a baking tray. Either brush the foil with oil or line with baking parchment.

2 Rinse the fish under running water and pat dry. Sprinkle with fennel seeds, salt and pepper and place on the lined baking tray. Oil another sheet of foil and use to make a tightly sealed but loose packet around the fish. Bake in the oven for 50 minutes.

3 Once cooked, leave in the foil for 10–15 minutes, then remove the head and peel away the skin (it comes away easily when the fish is still warm). You don't have to scrape away the brown meat, although this does improve the appearance.

4 Meanwhile, heat the oil and lightly fry the lemon slices. Use to garnish the fish, with the cherry tomatoes and parsley sprigs.

Golden saffron sauce

Saffron is the most expensive spice but adds an exquisite flavour and delicate colour to the crème fraîche.

SERVES 6

juice of ½ lemon
a pinch of saffron strands
450 ml (15 fl oz) crème fraîche
salt and freshly ground white pepper

1 Gently warm the lemon juice, add the saffron strands and leave to infuse for 10 minutes.

2 Strain the saffron liquor into the crème fraîche, season and stir well. Use the saffron strands to decorate the cream.

Saffron strands garnish our exotic saffron sauce.

Vegetable ribbons

There's no need to peel the courgettes before you make your ribbons as the skins will add to the colour and texture of the dish.

SERVES 6

4 carrots
4 courgettes
1 head of fennel
2 heads of chicory
75 g (3 oz) walnuts, chopped
2 tbsp black mustard seeds
6 tbsp vinaigrette dressing
2 tsp natural yoghurt
salt and freshly ground black pepper

1 Use a potato peeler to make ribbons out of the carrots and courgettes. Shred the fennel and chicory.

2 Toss all the ingredients together lightly, season well and serve.

Red rice and cucumber with mild chilli vinaigrette

Your should find red rice in major supermarkets or delicatessens, although you can substitute wild rice or other long-grain rice if you prefer.

SERVES 6

2 cucumbers
4 large eggs, hard-boiled
2 corn on the cob, cooked
150 g (5 oz) red rice, cooked
3 tbsp snipped fresh chives

FOR THE DRESSING

4 cm (1½ in) piece lemon grass, finely chopped
1 garlic clove, finely chopped
1 mild chilli pepper, finely chopped
6 tbsp good-quality vegetable oil
3 tbsp cider vinegar
a pinch of sugar
salt and freshly ground black pepper

1 Peel the cucumbers and cut into four lengthways. Discard the seeds and chop the flesh into small pieces.

2 Peel and chop the eggs and cut the corn away from the husks. Combine the cucumber, eggs, corn and cooked rice.

3 Place the lemon grass, garlic and chilli in a screw-topped jar with the oil, vinegar, sugar and seasoning and shake well.

4 Stir the dressing and chives into the salad, adjust the seasoning to taste and serve.

Pasta salad with golden pepper dressing

Peppers have a wonderful sweet flavour when cooked and add stunning colour to any dish. If you are really short of time, you can buy bottled peppers in the super-market, but they are only available in red!

SERVES 6

2 red peppers

2 orange peppers

2 yellow peppers

5 tbsp olive oil

250 g (9 oz) multi-coloured pasta shapes, cooked according to packet instructions

salt and freshly ground black pepper

3 tbsp roughly chopped fresh parsley

1 Preheat the oven to 180°C/350°F/gas mark 4.

2 Place the peppers on a baking tray, drizzle with a little of the oil and roast in the oven for about 20 minutes until the skin is wrinkled and slightly charred. Place in a plastic bag and leave to cool.

3 Peel off and discard the skins and seeds. Slice the flesh into strips.

4 Mix the red and orange peppers with the pasta.

5 To make the dressing, purée the yellow peppers with the remaining olive oil and a pinch of salt and pepper in a food processor. Stir into the pasta with the parsley, check and adjust the seasoning and serve.

Delicious summer salads (clockwise from front): vegetable ribbons, pasta salad with golden pepper dressing, red rice and cucumber with mild chilli vinaigrette.

29

Grand Marnier and apricot Alaska

The miracle of baked ice cream works because the meringue forms a seal around it, insulating it from the heat, so make sure you have no gaps in the meringue coating. Even if it does start to melt between oven and table, it will still taste delicious.

SERVES 6

- 1 litre (1¾ pints) firm vanilla ice cream (not soft scoop)
- 1 kg (2¼ lb) fresh apricots
- 1 x 200 g (7 oz) Madeira cake
- 5 tbsp Grand Marnier
- 3 egg whites
- 100 g (4 oz) caster sugar
- a few mint leaves
- a few redcurrants or other berries (optional)

1 Line a 900 g (2 lb) loaf tin with clingfilm. Using your hand and without allowing the ice cream to defrost, press the ice cream into the tin, leaving 2.5 cm (1 in) at the top for the cake. Place in the freezer for at least an hour so that the ice cream has become totally frozen again.

2 Stew the apricots with 1 tbsp of water in a pan for about 20 minutes until soft. The cooking time will depend on how ripe the fruit is. Unless the fruit is very tart there should be no need for sugar as the ice cream and meringue are so sweet.

3 Once cooked, allow to cool before discarding the stones and puréeing the flesh in a food processor.

4 Cut the cake into 2.5 cm (1 in) slices and use to cover the ice cream. Pour on the Grand Marnier and return to the freezer while you make the meringue.

5 Preheat the oven to 230°C/450°F/gas mark 8.

6 Whisk the egg whites until they form soft peaks, then add the sugar a tablespoon at a time and continue to whisk until the mixture is thick and glossy. Turn the ice cream out on to an ovenproof serving plate and completely cover it with meringue. Bake in the oven for 5 minutes or until just turning brown.

7 Garnish with mint leaves and serve immediately with a little purée on the serving dish and the remainder in a sauce boat. Garnish with a few bright berries for contrast, if liked.

Mango tarte tatin

Fresh mangoes give this familiar pudding a distinctive twist. Before turning out the tarte tatin, check that the pastry hasn't become stuck to the sides of the pan. If it has, place the pan on a gentle heat until the caramel has dissolved and the pastry loosened.

SERVES 6

4 tbsp caster sugar

4 medium-sized ripe mangoes, peeled and quartered

250 g (9 oz) puff pastry

300 ml (10 fl oz) double cream

1 Preheat the oven to 200°C/400°F/gas mark 6.

2 Dissolve the sugar in a large ovenproof frying pan and cook until it starts to turn golden.

3 Lay the mango quarters in the pan, rounded-side down and with the thin ends pointing towards the middle.

4 Roll out the pastry to 5 mm ($\frac{1}{4}$ in) thick and cut out a round slightly larger than the frying pan. Lay the pastry on top of the mangoes and tuck the pastry edges between the pan and the mangoes. Prick the centre of the pastry with a fork and bake in the oven for 20 minutes or until the pastry is cooked.

5 Remove from the oven and allow to cool slightly before placing a large plate on top of the pastry. Hold it securely and turn the frying pan over. Serve with plenty of double cream.

A variation on the usual tarte tatin, our version uses fresh mangoes instead of apples.

Midsummer Delight

Menu for twelve

STRAWBERRY PUNCH

—

HERBY MUSSELS

CHARGRILLED VEGETABLE TOASTS

CHICKEN FILOS

GRILLED PRAWNS

CHICKEN ALFRESCO

BABY BAKED POTATOES

CELERIAC, CARROT AND ORANGE SALAD

—

RASPBERRY CHARLOTTE

MELON GRANITA

*I*DEAL FOR *lunch on the very hottest days, this cold menu makes a glorious buffet spread. A collection of mini starters is perfect for eating with the fingers, and the creamy chicken main course is deliciously cooling. Finish with a chilled raspberry charlotte or glasses of crunchy melon granita.*

Strawberry punch

For a sophisticated opener, offer your guests this delicious drink on their arrival.

MAKES 24 GLASSES

900 g (2 lb) straw-
   berries, hulled
4 tbsp caster sugar
1 bottle dry white
   wine, chilled
about 20 ice cubes
3 bottles pink or
   rosé champagne
   or sparkling wine

1 Slice half the strawberries, place in a bowl with the sugar and mix well. Pour over the white wine, cover and chill for a few hours.

2 Strain the wine to remove the fruit, then pour it into a punch bowl. Halve the remaining straw-berries and add to the bowl with the ice cubes and cham-pagne or sparkling wine and serve at once.

Herby mussels

Always buy the freshest mussels you can find and, if you buy them raw, cook them on the day of purchase. Scrub and rinse them thoroughly, discarding any open ones, then place in a covered pan with a little water or wine over a high heat until they open, discarding any that remain closed.

MAKES 12

12 tbsp white breadcrumbs
4 tbsp chopped fresh parsley
2 garlic cloves, crushed
50 g (2 oz) butter, melted
freshly ground black pepper
12 New Zealand green-
   lipped mussels, cooked

1 Mix the breadcrumbs, parsley and garlic. Add enough melted butter to make a crumbly stuffing and season with black pepper.

2 Loosen the mussels from their shells, remov-ing the top shell. Cover each mussel with the crumb mix-ture and grill under a medium grill until the top-ping is golden.

Chargrilled vegetable toasts

The simplest of dishes are often the most effective – and delicious. Don't be misled by how easy this recipe is to prepare. It tastes wonderful.

SERVES 12

450 g (1 lb) aubergines

450 g (1 lb) red and yellow peppers

4 tbsp olive oil

salt and freshly ground black pepper

1 baguette

a few basil leaves

1 Preheat the oven to 220°C/425°F/gas mark 7.

2 Place the aubergines and peppers on a baking tray, drizzle with a little of the oil and roast in the oven for about 20 minutes until the skin is wrinkled and slightly charred. Place in a plastic bag and leave to cool.

3 Peel off and discard the skins and seeds from the peppers, then slice the flesh into thin strips. Remove the skins from the aubergines and dice the flesh. Add to the peppers with the remaining oil and season with salt and pepper.

4 Cut the baguette diagonally into 12 slices, then brush each slice with olive oil. Place on a baking tray and bake in the oven for 10 minutes.

5 Spoon the vegetables on to the bread, garnish with the basil leaves and serve.

Roses are at their best at this time of year, so choose a few fragrant blooms to decorate your table.

A summer spread (clockwise from bottom right): chargrilled vegetable toasts, herby mussels, olives, grilled prawns and chicken filos.

Chicken filos

These little pastry purses have a crisp outside and a deliciously moist filling. Prepare the filling in advance so that you have time to allow it to become quite cold before making the filos, and cover the pastry sheets you are not using with a damp tea towel to prevent them from drying out.

MAKES 12

225 g (8 oz) chicken livers

25 g (1 oz) butter

olive oil

1 garlic clove, crushed

4 juniper berries

a pinch of crushed dried red chilli peppers

1 heaped tsp chopped fresh thyme

2 tbsp brandy

salt and freshly ground black pepper

2 sheets ready-made filo pastry

1 Cut the chicken livers into bite-sized pieces. Heat the butter and ½ tsp of olive oil in a shallow pan. When the oil is very hot, stir-fry the livers briefly until just coloured. Add the garlic, juniper berries, chilli peppers and thyme and stir-fry for 1–2 minutes.

2 Add the brandy and cook over a very high heat, stirring constantly until the liquid has evaporated. Season and set aside until cold.

3 Preheat the oven to 200°C/400°F/gas mark 6.

4 To make the filo parcels, brush the pastry with olive oil, place one sheet on top of the other, then fold in half to form a rectangle. Cut lengthways into six equal pieces, then cut each one in half.

5 Place a little of the filling in the centre of each pastry piece, brush the surrounding pastry with oil, then gather the edges together, twisting the top to form a pouch.

6 Brush with oil and place on an oiled baking sheet. Bake in the oven for 10 minutes until crisp and golden.

Chicken alfresco

This makes a stunning buffet centrepiece, served with fresh figs, vegetables and a tasty dressing.

SERVES 12

2 x 1.6 kg (3½ lb) free-range chickens, skinned
1 litre (1¾ pints) dry white wine
2 small onions, studded with cloves
4 celery sticks, sliced
20 black peppercorns
a few tarragon sprigs
salt and freshly ground black pepper
2 avocados, peeled, stoned and roughly chopped
10 sun-dried tomatoes, finely chopped
1 garlic clove, crushed
3 tbsp mayonnaise
juice of ½ lemon
8 basil leaves, shredded
50 g (2 oz) pine nuts, lightly toasted

TO SERVE

550 g (1¼ lb) French beans
550 g (1¼ lb) asparagus spears
6–8 ripe figs, halved
tiny cherry tomatoes
a few basil leaves

FOR THE DRESSING

8 tbsp olive oil
4 tbsp tarragon vinegar
150 ml (5 fl oz) Greek yoghurt
2 tbsp snipped fresh chives
½ tbsp chopped fresh tarragon

1 Put the chickens in two lidded pans and pour over the wine. Add just enough water almost to cover the chickens. Bring to the boil over a medium heat.

2 Divide the onions, celery, peppercorns and tarragon between the pans and season with salt. Cover tightly and simmer over a very low heat for 45 minutes. Remove from the heat and leave the chickens to cool in the stock.

3 When cool, remove the dark meat from the wings, legs and back of the chickens. Dice all the brown meat and mix thoroughly with the avocado, sun-dried tomatoes, garlic, mayonnaise, lemon juice and shredded basil leaves. Season and mix thoroughly, then stir in half the toasted pine nuts.

4 Spoon the mixture into a bowl or basin lined with clingfilm. Press the mixture down and smooth the surface. Chill thoroughly.

5 Steam or boil the French beans and asparagus until *al dente.*

6 Mix together the dressing ingredients.

7 Turn the brown meat mixture out on to a large serving platter and decorate with the rest of the pine nuts. Slice the white meat and arrange around the brown meat mixture with the cooked vegetables and halved figs. Decorate with cherry tomatoes and basil leaves. Serve with the dressing.

Baby baked potatoes

When you have plenty to do, keep your vegetable preparation simple. If you like garlic, add a crushed clove or two to the oil for extra flavour.

SERVES 12

1.5 kg (3 lb) small new potatoes
150 ml (5 fl oz) olive oil
salt and freshly ground black pepper
5 rosemary sprigs

1 Preheat the oven to 200°C/400°F/gas mark 6.

2 Scrub the potatoes well and divide between five double sheets of foil. Add 2 tbsp of olive oil, salt, pepper and a rosemary sprig to each one. Fold into loose parcels. Bake in the oven for 1¼–1½ hours until tender.

Celeriac, carrot and orange salad

This unusual combination of flavours is tangy and refreshing.

SERVES 12

5 large carrots, coarsely grated
1 celeriac root, coarsely grated
3 large oranges, peeled and chopped
juice of 1 lemon
2 tbsp olive oil
1 tbsp snipped fresh chives

1 Mix the carrots, celeriac and oranges.

2 Toss with the lemon juice and olive oil, season with snipped chives and serve.

Chicken alfresco served with asparagus and french beans, salad and fresh bread.

Raspberry charlotte

A perfect party pudding that makes the most of summer raspberries.

SERVES 12

700 g (1½ lb) fresh raspberries

50 g (2 oz) icing sugar, sifted, plus extra for dusting

50 ml (2 fl oz) water

1½ sachets of powdered gelatine

3 tbsp Kirsch

500 g (18 oz) ready-made custard

175 ml (6 fl oz) whipping cream

2 Swiss rolls

a few mint leaves

1 Reserve a few raspberries for decoration. Crush the remainder, mix with the icing sugar and set aside.

2 Place the water in a small bowl and sprinkle over the gelatine. Stand the bowl in a pan of gently simmering water and leave to dissolve, stirring occasionally. Remove from the heat and add the Kirsch.

3 Gently fold together the sugared fruit, gelatine mixture and custard. Whip the cream until it just holds its shape, then fold into the custard mixture.

4 Line a 20 cm (8 in) loose-bottomed or spring-form cake tin with clingfilm. Cut the Swiss rolls into 1.5 cm (½ in) slices and use to line the base and sides of the tin. Spoon the filling into the centre. Cover with clingfilm and chill until set.

5 To serve, trim off any excess pieces of sponge and turn the charlotte out on to a serving plate. Decorate with the reserved raspberries and the mint leaves and dust with a little icing sugar.

Melon granita

The perfect end to a summer meal, this crystallized water ice is a classic Italian dessert which can be served with brandy snaps or your favourite dessert biscuits.

SERVES 12

1.75 kg (4 lb) very ripe galia or ogen melons

juice of 1 large lemon

65 g (2½ oz) caster sugar

2–3 tbsp orange flower water

a few strawberries, halved

TO SERVE

brandy snaps or dessert biscuits

1 Peel and seed the melons, then cut the flesh into chunks and process in a blender until it forms a smooth purée.

2 Stir together the lemon juice and sugar until the sugar has dissolved. Mix with the fruit pulp and flavour with the orange flower water.

3 Pour the mixture into two freezer containers and freeze until solid.

4 Scrape the granita with a fork until it has a snow-like texture, then process it briefly again in batches. Return to the freezer until ready to serve. The granita will keep its snow-like texture and can be served straight from the freezer.

5 Decorate with strawberry halves and serve with dessert biscuits.

Holiday Special

RECAPTURE YOUR *holiday memories, from crispy garlic chicken to freshly picked summer fruit. We've mixed Middle Eastern, Mediterranean and classic English flavours for the ultimate easy-living menu.*

THE PERFECT PIMM'S
The ultimate summer drink, Pimm's is deliciously refreshing and deceptively potent! Here's the definitive recipe. Take a chilled tall glass or jug and fill one-third full with ice. For each measure of Pimm's No.1 Cup, add three measures of lemonade. Stir gently before garnishing with orange, lemon, cucumber and strawberry plus a sprig of mint or borage.

Menu for six

PIMM'S

—

FALAFELS WITH SESAME SLAW
AND YOGHURT AND CHILLI DIP

—

GRILLED BABY COURGETTES
AND AUBERGINES

SPICY SUMMER CHICKEN

TOMATO AND SPRING ONION
CRACKED WHEAT SALAD

GARLIC AND HERB DRESSING

CRISPY CRUDITÉS

—

PASSION FRUIT AND LIME MOUSSE WITH
WHITE CHOCOLATE SAUCE

SUMMER PUDDING WITH ROSE PETAL CREAM

SETTING THE SCENE
Capturing the mood when you're eating alfresco means creating a relaxed and informal table setting, so avoid delicate tableware and hard-to-wash table linens: keep your presentation as simple as possible.

Falafels and sesame slaw with yoghurt and chilli dip

A Middle Eastern snack, falafels make delicious starters. They are great for entertaining as they can be made in advance and reheated when you need them.

SERVES 6

FOR THE FALAFELS

225 g (8 oz) tinned chick peas

1 small potato, peeled and grated

3 garlic cloves, grated

1 small strong onion, finely chopped

1 tbsp tahini paste

2 tsp ground cumin

1 tsp crushed dried chilli peppers

$\frac{1}{2}$ tsp salt

2 tbsp instant mashed potato

2 tbsp chopped fresh coriander

oil for deep-frying

FOR THE COLESLAW

100 g (4 oz) white cabbage, shredded

100 g (4 oz) red cabbage, shredded

1 red onion, shredded

2 tsp tahini paste

3 tsp sesame seeds, toasted

6 tbsp olive oil dressing

TO SERVE

150 ml (5 fl oz) natural organic yoghurt

1 little gem lettuce

6 tsp hot chilli sauce

1 Rinse the chick peas, then drain and dry on kitchen paper. Roughly pound them, using a potato masher.

2 Mix in all the remaining ingredients except the frying oil and blend well.

3 Before frying the falafels, test their consistency by heating the oil to medium-hot. Drop in a teaspoonful of the mixture and cook for 1–2 minutes, turning gently with a slotted spoon. Remove and drain. If the falafel comes apart, add more instant potato to the mixture until it binds together.

4 Shape into about 12 thick burger shapes and fry in a shallow pan for 2–3 minutes in medium-hot oil, turning with the slotted spoon until cooked through and golden.

5 Toss the cabbage and onion in the tahini, sesame seeds and dressing, and serve in little gem leaves along with the falafels, yoghurt and chilli.

6 Divide the yoghurt between six lettuce leaves and spoon the chilli sauce into the centre.

Grilled baby courgettes and aubergines

The quantities you cook for this dish will depend on the size of the vegetables so adapt them accordingly. You may also need to adjust the cooking time.

SERVES 6

6–12 baby courgettes

6–12 baby aubergines

olive oil

1 tbsp chopped fresh thyme

salt and freshly ground black pepper

1 Brush the vegetables fairly generously with olive oil, then season with thyme, salt and pepper.

2 Cook for 5–10 minutes either on a barbecue or under a medium-hot grill, turning occasionally. When soft and lightly browned, sprinkle with a little more salt, pepper and thyme before serving.

Spicy summer chicken

A light, simple dish that can be barbecued or oven cooked.

SERVES 6

$\frac{1}{2}$ tsp ground cinnamon

$\frac{1}{2}$ tsp ground allspice

$\frac{1}{2}$ tsp ground black pepper

2 garlic cloves, crushed

175 ml (6 fl oz) natural yoghurt

6 chicken quarters on the bone

olive oil

salt

1 Stir the spices, pepper and garlic into the yoghurt, then rub the mixture into the chicken. Marinate for at least an hour.

2 Preheat the oven to 200°C/400°F/gas mark 6.

3 Drizzle the chicken with a little olive oil and sprinkle with salt before cooking in the oven for 30 minutes. Alternatively cook on a barbecue for 20 minutes each side.

Tomato and spring onion cracked wheat salad

Burghul, bulgar or cracked wheat – it goes by several names – comes from North Africa. It's deliciously tasty in a salad and also highly nutritious.

SERVES 6

100 g (4 oz) cracked wheat (burghul)

175 g (6 oz) large bunch of flatleaf parsley with stalks, finely shredded

175 g (6 oz) bunch of mint with stalks, finely shredded

5 salad tomatoes, finely chopped

4 spring onions, finely chopped

150 ml (5 fl oz) olive oil

juice of 1 lemon

salt and freshly ground black pepper

1 Rinse the wheat and place in a bowl. Just cover with boiling water, allowing enough to be absorbed by the wheat. Leave for 30 minutes, then drain well.

2 Stir in the remaining ingredients and season to taste.

Creamy garlic and coriander salad dressing works perfectly with the flavours of the chicken and salad.

Garlic and herb dressing

This is really worth making if you have the time.

SERVES 6

3 large garlic cloves

a handful of coriander leaves

1 egg yolk

120 ml (4 fl oz) olive oil

4 tbsp natural yoghurt

salt and freshly ground black pepper

1 Put the garlic and coriander leaves into a food processor and process until roughly chopped.

2 Add the egg yolk, then turn the processor up to full speed and drizzle in the olive oil. Stir in the yoghurt and season to taste.

Crispy crudités

This makes the ultimate no-fuss salad – if you use bite-sized ingredients, you don't even need to chop them. Choose a mixture of salad vegetables such as cherry tomatoes, spring onions, radishes, Chinese leaves, crisp salad leaves, aiming for a variety of shape, colour and texture. If you want to include larger vegetables such as peppers or courgettes, just cut them into pieces.

Having washed and prepared the vegetables, simply lay the ingredients on a flat serving dish and sprinkle with water. Place the dish inside a large, airtight plastic bag. Chill for 30 minutes before serving with good quality mayonnaise or garlic and herb dressing.

Summer pudding with rose petal cream

The most English of summer desserts

SERVES 6

300 ml (10 fl oz) water
50 g (2 oz) caster sugar
750 g (1¾ lb) summer fruit such as blackberries, redcurrants, raspberries, blackcurrants or strawberries, cut into small pieces
5–7 thin slices of white bread
mint leaves and rose petals
1 large carton double cream or Greek yoghurt
2–3 tsp rose water

1 Place the water and sugar in a large pan and stir over a low heat until the sugar has dissolved and the syrup is hot.

2 Reserve some fruit for garnish. Add the rest of the fruit to the hot syrup, stirring gently to coat. Remove from the heat.

3 Cut the crusts off the bread and use to line a greased medium-sized pudding basin.

4 Using a slotted spoon, transfer the fruit to the pudding basin, lay a slice of bread on top and cover with clingfilm. Put a small plate or saucer and weight on top to press the juices through the bread. Keep any remaining fruit and juices for decoration. Chill overnight.

5 Turn on to a serving plate. Spoon over a little of the reserved juice and decorate with fruit, mint leaves and rose petals.

6 Lightly whip the double cream or Greek yoghurt, flavour with a few teaspoons of rose water and serve in a separate dish.

Passion fruit and lime mousse with white chocolate sauce

A seriously indulgent dessert, this takes advantage of the unusual fruits now available.

SERVES 6

12 passion fruit
6 limes
50 g (2 oz) caster sugar
1 tsp powdered gelatine
300 ml (10 fl oz) double cream
2 egg whites
a few mint leaves

FOR THE SAUCE

175 g (6 oz) white chocolate
6 tbsp double cream

1 Halve and reserve 3 passion fruit; remove the flesh from the remainder. Cut 2 limes into wedges and reserve. Zest and juice the remaining limes.

2 Combine two-thirds of the passion fruit flesh with the lime zest and caster sugar.

3 Gently heat the lime juice, add the gelatine and stir until dissolved. Leave to cool slightly.

4 Lightly whip the cream, then fold in the passion fruit and lime zest mixture and the cooled lime juice.

5 Whisk the egg whites until they form soft peaks, then, using a large metal spoon, fold into the cream. Turn into a bowl and chill for 1 hour.

6 Make the sauce just before serving. Very gently melt the chocolate in a heatproof bowl over a pan of barely simmering water. Heat the cream to scalding point and gently stir into the chocolate. Set aside.

7 To serve each mousse, place a large spoon point-down into the mixture and turn 360 degrees to cut out a cone. Turn out on to a plate.

8 Serve with a spoonful of the remaining passion fruit flesh. Decorate with the reserved passion fruit halves, the lime wedges and mint leaves. The chocolate sauce can be served separately or poured on top.

Above left: *Summer pudding.*

Right: *Passion fruit and lime mousse.*

Winter

Warmers

ENTERING REALLY comes into its own during the winter months when there's nothing nicer than lighting the fire, shutting out the cold and enjoying good food and the company of friends. And the food couldn't be easier. Take your pick from this delicious selection of elegant dinners, casual suppers and weekend lunches.

Foolproof Dinner Party

I F YOU *thought soufflé and crème brûlée were best left to the professionals, this is the menu to change your mind. These foolproof recipes are designed to leave the cook feeling smug – and the guests thoroughly impressed!*

Menu for six

PISSALADIÈRE

COURGETTE SOUFFLÉ

—

BOEUF EN CROUTE

—

CRÈME BRÛLÉE

CARAMEL SWIRLS

BITTER CHOCOLATE AND ALMOND GÂTEAU

TRUFFLE CURLS

SETTING THE SCENE
Special meals need special table settings. There's nothing to beat classic combinations like cream and gold china against damask table linen

Pissaladière

A light and colourful tart served cut into slices. If you use frozen puff pastry, make sure it is thawed completely before use – or you might like to make your own (see page 45).

SERVES 6

2 tbsp olive oil
2 onions, sliced
200 g (7 oz) puff pastry
4–6 tbsp tomato purée
50 g (2 oz) tin of anchovies
100 g (4 oz) stoned black
    olives
1 tbsp chopped fresh thyme

1 Preheat the oven to 180°C/350°F/gas mark 4.

2 Heat the oil and fry the onions until soft.

3 Roll the pastry into 5 cm (2 in) wide strips and prick all over with a fork.

4 Spread the tomato purée over the pastry, not quite to the edges.

5 Cover with the onions, then lay the anchovies and olives on top to form a symmetrical pattern.

6 Sprinkle with thyme and cook in the oven for 15–20 minutes. Serve warm.

Courgette soufflé

A classic that isn't half as difficult as people think. The trick is organization, so get everything you need prepared in advance. A small soufflé will hold for no more than a minute, so make sure your guests are ready and waiting at the table. If your soufflé does collapse, don't worry – it will still taste delicious.

SERVES 6

25 g (1 oz) butter, plus extra for greasing

450 g (1 lb) courgettes, chopped

38 g (1¼ oz) plain flour

150 ml (5 fl oz) milk

75 g (3 oz) strong Cheddar cheese, finely grated

5 large eggs, separated (only 3 yolks are used)

freshly grated nutmeg

salt and freshly ground black pepper

1 First prepare the ramekins by greasing the insides thoroughly with melted butter.

2 To make paper collars, cut out six strips of silicone paper double in thickness and long enough to wrap around the ramekins. Dampen the paper, if necessary, to make it easier to handle. Tie the collars around the outside of the ramekins with cooks' string or thin wire (wire is easier to deal with), ensuring that there is 4 cm (1½ in) of paper above the rim of each ramekin. Put the ramekins on a baking tray.

3 Arrange the oven so there's plenty of rising room, then preheat to 200°C/400°F/gas mark 6.

4 Steam the courgettes for 10 minutes, then process to a rough purée. Place in a fine strainer to drain away surplus liquid.

5 Put the butter, flour and milk in a pan and cook over a low heat, stirring with a whisk until thickened. Add most of the cheese, the courgette purée and 3 egg yolks. Season with nutmeg, salt and pepper.

6 In a clean, dry, grease-free bowl, whisk all the egg whites. Start gently and gradually increase to full speed until they hold stiff peaks.

7 Stir a little egg white into the courgette mixture to soften it, then, using a large metal spoon, gently fold in the remaining egg white. Quickly spoon the soufflé into the prepared ramekins up to the rim.

8 Sprinkle the tops with the remaining cheese and cook in the oven for 18–20 minutes. The tops will go nicely brown and the centre of the soufflé will be a little runny. Use scissors to cut the string or wire and peel away the paper, then serve the soufflés immediately.

Boeuf en croûte

A classic with a twist: in our version, smoked ham and cooked spinach are used to wrap the beef. Serve it with julienned vegetables and gravy flavoured with a dash of port.

SERVES 6

900 g (2 lb) rolled beef fillet
salt and freshly ground
   black pepper
2 tsp chopped fresh thyme
2 tsp strong mustard
550 g (1¼ lb) puff pastry
8 large slices smoked,
   cooked ham
100 g (4 oz) spinach,
   chopped, cooked and
   well drained
1 egg, beaten

1 Quickly seal the meat in a hot frying pan, then season, sprinkle with thyme and spread with mustard.

2 Roll out the pastry long and wide enough to wrap the meat completely. You will need to allow a 2 cm (¾ in) overlap for the seal.

Serve your beef with light vegetables, such as slivers of lightly cooked carrot, leek and courgette.

3 Lay four slices of ham in the centre of the pastry and place half the spinach on top of this, followed by the beef. Put the remaining spinach and ham on top of the beef (it doesn't matter if a little spinach escapes or the ham doesn't form a perfect seal).

4 Use one hand to hold the ham and spinach on to the beef and the other to wrap the pastry around the beef as tightly as possible. Brush the two edges with beaten egg and place the beef, seal-side down, on to a greased baking tray. Chill for at least an hour.

5 Preheat the oven to 230°C/450°F/gas mark 8.

6 Cook the beef for 20–30 minutes for medium rare or 35–40 minutes for well done. Cover with foil if the pastry is becoming too dark before the meat is ready.

Home-made puff pastry

Here's the definitive puff pastry recipe. Although it is time-consuming, it's worth making for a really special meal.

MAKES 1 KG (2¼ LB)

450 g (1 lb) strong plain flour
1 tsp salt
175 ml (6 fl oz) cold water
450 g (1 lb) unsalted butter,
   at room temperature

1 Sift the flour and salt on to a work surface, make a well in the centre and add the water and 60 g (2¼ oz) of the butter.

2 Using your fingers, work into a dough ball, cover with clingfilm and chill for at least 30 minutes.

3 On a lightly floured surface, roll out the dough into a 20 cm (8 in) square. The corners should be rolled a little thinner at the edges than the centre.

4 Shape the remaining butter into a block that will fit into the centre of the pastry, and bring the four corners of pastry up over the butter to make a neat, tight parcel. Pinch the edges to seal them. If the butter is starting to ooze, chill the pastry for 15 minutes.

5 Roll out into a strip three times as long as it is wide. If the pastry breaks and the butter is exposed, take dough from the edges to patch it up. Fold the bottom third of the rectangle up and the top third down over the top, then turn the pastry 90 degrees.

6 Repeat the rolling, folding and turning, always turning in the same direction. Don't use too much flour. When two turns have been completed, wrap the pastry in clingfilm and chill for 1 hour or overnight.

7 The pastry needs to be rolled, folded and turned twice again and rested for another hour.

FINISHING TOUCHES
If you're keeping the table setting stylishly restrained, you can afford to add flashes of bolder colour with flowers and accessories. For a really rich, wintry effect, mix seasonal berries with variegated foliage.

8 If you have any thin areas where the butter is seeping through, patch them with pastry. The pastry needs two more turns (making six in total) and another hour-long rest before it is ready to be rolled out and used.

Crème brûlée

A sublime dessert, crème brûlée requires an eagle eye – so don't walk away while it's on the stove. It's traditionally served in ramekins with burnt sugar on top. Instead we put dessertspoonfuls ('quenelles' in chef speak) on to dessert plates and served it with caramel swirls and fruit dipped in caramel.

SERVES 6

6 egg yolks
4 tbsp caster sugar
450 ml (15 fl oz) double
  cream
1 tsp vanilla essence

1 Start by getting ready a large pan, a bowl or a jug with a fine sieve resting on top, a small balloon whisk and a sink full of cold water.

2 Beat the egg yolks and sugar together until pale and thick. Put the cream and vanilla essence into the pan and gently heat to just before boiling point. Pour the hot cream over the eggs while gently mixing with a balloon whisk. Don't create too much froth.

3 Return the mixture to the pan and place on a low heat. Use a wooden spoon to stir the mixture gently but constantly and scrape it around the edges and bottom of the pan. Don't walk away from the stove!

4 As the custard gets near to boiling point, remove from the heat. At this stage it should easily coat the back of a spoon. If it looks too thin, return the mixture to the stove and continue to cook. Once thick, rest the pan in the sink of cold water to prevent further cooking, then quickly pour through the sieve into the bowl. Allow to cool before chilling overnight.

Caramel swirls

These make elegant decorations for your desserts. You can crush leftovers and serve as an ice cream topping. Quantities are not crucial, but these amounts will give you a guide. You will need to work quite quickly and be very careful not to touch the hot caramel. If it becomes too hard to work with, simply return it to the hob and heat gently.

SERVES 6

450 g (1 lb) caster sugar
300 ml (10 fl oz) water

1 Cover the bottom of a pan with the sugar and add enough water so you can move your finger in the sugar. Cook over a medium heat and stir the mixture gently with a wooden spoon to dissolve.

2 Once the sugar has dissolved, use a wet pastry brush to remove any sugar from the sides of the pan. Stop stirring and increase the heat slightly. Bring to the boil and cook until the syrup is honey gold in colour. Prevent any further cooking by quickly resting the pan in a sink full of cold water.

Our wonderfully rich crème brûlée is flavoured with vanilla, topped with caramel swirls and served with fresh figs.

3 Allow the syrup to cool slightly before using a spoon to drizzle the caramel on to silicone paper. Once hardened, the swirls can be used as decorations.

4 Dip seedless grapes or pieces of fruit in the remaining caramel and use as an accompaniment to the crème brûlée.

For a really rich, wintry effect, mix seasonal berries with variegated foliage.

Bitter chocolate and almond gâteau

A real indulgence that will endear you to all chocolate lovers. Always choose the best-quality bitter chocolate with at least 70 per cent cocoa solids.

SERVES 6

250 g (9 oz) good-quality
    plain chocolate
250 g (9 oz) butter
250 g (9 oz) caster sugar
6 large eggs
250 g (9 oz) ground
    almonds
300 ml (10 fl oz) double
    cream, whipped
icing sugar, sifted
truffle curls

1 Preheat the oven to 160°C/350°F/gas mark 4 and line a square tin or small, deep baking tray with silicone paper.

2 Melt the chocolate in a heatproof bowl over a pan of barely simmering water.

3 Cream the butter and sugar until light and fluffy, then add the melted chocolate. Stir well.

4 Add the eggs one at a time, then fold in the almonds. Pour into the tin and bake in the oven for 35 minutes.

5 Allow to cool, then cut into squares. Slice each square in half horizontally and fill with whipped cream. Dust with icing sugar and serve with a truffle curl on top.

Truffle curls

These are a delicious decoration for the gâteau, or can be used on cakes or ice cream. Any leftover truffle mixture can be frozen and used on another occasion.

SERVES 6

150 ml (5 fl oz) double cream
150 g (5 oz) good-quality
    plain chocolate

1 Bring the double cream to the boil, add the chocolate and stir over a low heat until melted. Pour into a flat dish and chill for at least 2 hours.

2 Slightly warm a dessert-spoon and drag it along the mixture to form a curl. Put the curl straight on to baking paper and pop into the freezer to firm up before serving with the gâteau.

Saturday Night Supper

T HE BEAUTY of this menu is its simplicity. Freshly cooked mussels are always a treat, and here they're followed by a spicy aubergine and olive Italian pasta dish and, for dessert, a deliciously different bread and butter pudding flavoured with nuts and spices.

Menu for six

SPICY THAI MUSSELS

—

SPAGHETTI CAPONATA

—

GROWN-UP
BREAD AND BUTTER PUDDING

Spicy Thai mussels

Always buy mussels on the day you plan to eat them, clean them thoroughly and be ruthless in discarding any that do not behave as they should (see method). If you don't have a large enough pan, cook the mussels in two batches. Serve with plenty of crusty bread to mop up the juices.

SERVES 6

- 2.75 kg (6 lb) fresh mussels in their shells
- 50 ml (2 fl oz) corn oil
- 8 shallots or 1 red onion, chopped
- 4 garlic cloves, finely chopped
- 4 cm ($1\frac{1}{2}$ in) piece of root ginger, finely chopped
- 3 pieces lemon grass, cut into 2.5 cm (1 in) lengths
- 175 ml (6 fl oz) water
- 200 g (7 oz) jar of hot and spicy tomato sauce
- 1 lime or lemon, cut into wedges

1 Place the mussels in a large bowl of cold water. Scrub the shells thoroughly with a vegetable brush and scrape off any barnacles with a small knife.

2 Transfer the mussels to clean water and scrub thoroughly a second time. Pull off any beard-like threads. Rinse under cold running water. Discard any mussels with broken shells and any open mussels that do not close firmly when tapped sharply with a knife.

3 Heat the oil in a large shallow pan with a well-fitting lid. Sauté the shallots or onion, garlic, ginger and lemon grass for 3–4 minutes. Add the water and tomato sauce and bring to the boil.

4 Add the mussels, cover and cook for 5–6 minutes, shaking the pan vigorously and often. The mussels should now have opened; discard any which remain closed.

5 Transfer the mussels and sauce to a large, warmed serving dish and garnish with lime or lemon wedges.

Spaghetti caponata

Authentic Sicilian caponata is a sweet and sour aubergine salad. With a few additions, it becomes a delicious hot, spicy pasta sauce that's very easy to make. To toast the pine nuts, toss them in a hot, dry frying pan for a few minutes, shaking the pan all the time, until they are lightly speckled brown. A crisp mixed salad makes a good accompaniment to the dish.

SERVES 6

900 g (2 lb) aubergines, cut in 1 cm ($\frac{1}{2}$ in) cubes

salt and freshly ground black pepper

$\frac{1}{2}$ fennel bulb, thinly sliced

5 tbsp olive oil

1 red onion, thinly sliced

3 garlic cloves, crushed

65 g (2$\frac{1}{2}$ oz) small stoned black or green olives

1 heaped tbsp capers, chopped

400 g (14 oz) tin of peeled tomatoes, chopped

3–4 tbsp balsamic vinegar

a large pinch of brown sugar

50 g (2 oz) tin of anchovy fillets, drained and chopped

3 tbsp fresh flatleaf parsley, chopped

3 tbsp pine kernels, toasted

TO SERVE

700–750 g (1$\frac{1}{2}$ –1$\frac{3}{4}$ lb) fresh spaghetti or tagliatelle, boiled in plenty of salted water until *al dente*

Parmesan cheese, freshly grated

1 Place the aubergines in a colander and sprinkle with salt. Set aside for 1 hour. As well as drawing out the bitter juices, this process also means less oil is needed for cooking. Rinse thoroughly and dry on kitchen paper.

2 Blanch the sliced fennel in boiling water for about 2 minutes, then drain.

3 Heat the oil in a large, heavy pan and add the aubergines, fennel, onion and garlic. Sauté for 10–12 minutes, stirring often.

4 Add the olives, capers, tomatoes, vinegar and sugar. Season with plenty of pepper. Cover the pan and simmer for 15–20 minutes or until the aubergines are soft.

5 Stir in the anchovies and parsley. Check the seasoning.

6 Arrange the cooked pasta on a large, warmed serving platter. Spoon the sauce into the centre and scatter with the toasted pine kernels. Toss the pasta at the table and serve with freshly grated Parmesan cheese.

Grown-up bread and butter pudding

This is a grown-up version of the classic nursery pudding. Put it in the oven when you sit down to eat your starter and it will be ready at just the right time. Although best eaten freshly baked, it is still delicious if baked in advance, then covered with foil and reheated for 20 minutes at 180°C/ 350°F/ gas mark 4.

SERVES 6

750 ml (1$\frac{1}{4}$ pints) single cream

6 large eggs, separated

75 g (3 oz) caster sugar

40 ml (1$\frac{1}{2}$ fl oz) dark rum

50 g (2 oz) unsalted butter

175 g (6 oz) sliced brioche or other fresh white bread, crusts removed

40 g (1$\frac{1}{2}$ oz) raisins

40 g (1$\frac{1}{2}$ oz) pecan nuts, roughly chopped

1 heaped tsp ground cinnamon

1 Pour the cream into a pan and heat to a simmer. Remove from the heat.

2 Whisk the egg yolks with the sugar and rum until light and fluffy. Pour in the cream a little at a time, whisking continuously.

3 Grease an ovenproof gratin or pie dish. Butter one side of the bread slices and halve diagonally. Place a layer of bread, butter-side up, in the prepared dish and sprinkle with some of the raisins and nuts. Repeat the layers, finishing with a layer of bread.

4 Pour the custard through a strainer over the pudding and leave to stand for 20 minutes.

5 Preheat the oven to 190°C/375°F/gas mark 5.

SETTING THE SCENE
Chunky continental-style tableware is ideal for a casual meal and suits the rustic flavour of this menu. Fresh flowers provide instant table dressing. There's no need for an elaborate arrangement – an earthenware pitcher is simple but effective.

6 Dust the pudding with cinnamon and place in a large roasting tin. Fill the tin with hot water to come half way up the sides of the dish. Bake in the oven for 40–45 minutes until the pudding is just set and golden brown. Serve warm.

Crisp and Classic

ROAST LAMB is always a favourite, and our crispy, Greek-style version is almost impossible to overcook, so it's perfect for when you don't know exactly what time your guests will arrive. With a warm salad and a choice of irresistible puddings, it is a simply delicious choice for any occasion.

Warm vegetable salad with dill dressing

Use ready-prepared salad with a good mix of interesting leaves to minimize preparation time. French bread crostini make an excellent accompaniment to this salad. Just thinly slice the bread at an angle, drizzle with olive oil and bake in a hot oven for a few minutes until crisp and pale brown.

SERVES 6

250 g (9 oz) asparagus

200 g (7 oz) patty pan squash

2 large leeks

1 cucumber

3 courgettes or 9 baby courgettes

200 g (7 oz) fine green beans

3 eggs, hard-boiled

100 g (4 oz) mixed salad leaves

6 radishes, sliced

FOR THE DRESSING

2 tbsp chopped fresh dill

1 tsp Dijon mustard

2 tbsp red wine vinegar

2 tbsp sunflower oil

2 tbsp olive oil

a pinch of caster sugar

salt and freshly ground black pepper

1 To prepare the vegetables, wash them thoroughly. Trim away the tough part of the asparagus stalks. Cut the squash in half and the leeks into strips. Peel the cucumber and the courgettes (baby courgettes don't need peeling) and cut into little fingers. Trim the green beans.

2 Separate the hard-boiled eggs into yolk and white and grate with a fine cheese grater.

3 Place all the dressing ingredients into a screw-topped jar and shake vigorously.

4 Steam or boil the vegetables for 3 minutes, then drain. Place the warm vegetables in a large bowl with the salad leaves. Add the dressing and toss thoroughly. Sprinkle the egg on top, garnish with radishes and serve immediately.

Greek-style roast leg of lamb

In this recipe, the lamb is cooked for a long time so that it falls off the bone. It's almost impossible to overdo, but you may need to add a little more wine if you leave it for longer than the specified cooking time.

SERVES 6

1 x 1.5–1.75 kg (3–4 lb) leg of lamb

4 large garlic cloves, cut into slivers

2 tbsp olive oil

2 tbsp dried oregano

salt and freshly ground black pepper

about 300 ml (10 fl oz) dry white wine

a squeeze of lemon juice (optional)

1 Preheat the oven to 200°C/400°F/gas mark 6.

2 Cut small slits all over the lamb and insert slivers of garlic. Mix the olive oil, oregano and a generous grinding of black pepper. Using your hand, rub the mixture all over the lamb, then sprinkle with salt.

3 Place the lamb in a large roasting tin and pour in enough wine to cover the base. Roast in the oven for 20 minutes, then reduce the oven temperature to 180°C/350°F/gas mark 4 and cook for a further 2 hours. Allow the lamb to rest for 15 minutes before carving.

4 Skim most of the fat from the juices left in the tin and whisk in a splash more wine or a squeeze of lemon juice. Reheat the sauce and serve separately.

SETTING THE SCENE
Crisp white table linen is the perfect backdrop for any colour scheme and has just enough formality to create a sense of occasion. Pale blue is a wonderful colour against which to display food – these plates look great with both savoury and sweet courses.

Grilled red onions

Red onions have a slightly sweeter flavour than traditional onions and offer a wonderful colour contrast with the rest of the menu.

SERVES 6

6 red onions, halved
olive oil
salt and freshly ground
    black pepper

1 Place the onion halves in a grill pan, drizzle generously with the oil and season with salt and pepper.

2 Grill under a medium grill for 10 minutes until tender and golden brown.

Slow-cooked lamb flavoured with wine, garlic and lemon juice is served with grilled red onions and crispy potatoes cooked with stock and tomato.

Crispy fondant potatoes

It is best to peel the potatoes for this recipe before cooking them.

SERVES 6

12 medium-sized potatoes
1 vegetable stock cube
1 tbsp tomato purée
50 g (2 oz) butter, melted
salt and freshly ground
    black pepper

1 Preheat the oven to 180°C/350°F/gas mark 4.

2 Cut the potatoes in half, place them in a large pan and cover with water. Crumble in the stock cube, add the tomato purée and bring to the boil, then simmer for 10 minutes.

3 With a slotted spoon, transfer the potatoes to a roasting tin and gently score the top side of each potato with a fork. Pour enough of the tomato stock into the tin to submerge half of each potato. Spoon a little melted butter over each potato, then sprinkle with salt and pepper.

4 Cook in the oven for 45 minutes. Use any remaining tomato stock to top up the roasting tin towards the end of the cooking time. The tops of the potatoes will turn crisp and golden.

Double chocolate sponge puddings

Line the basins with microwave-proof clingfilm to make turning out easy. If you don't have individual moulds, use heatproof ceramic cups. Our bitter chocolate sauce makes the ideal accompaniment.

SERVES 6

150 g (5 oz) self-raising flour
25 g (1 oz) cocoa powder
175 g (6 oz) butter
175 g (6 oz) caster sugar
3 large eggs
1 tsp vanilla essence
50 g (2 oz) plain chocolate chips
1 tbsp hot water
a few redcurrants
a few mint sprigs

1 Sift the flour and cocoa into a bowl.

2 In another bowl, cream the butter and sugar until light and fluffy, then gradually beat in the eggs and add the vanilla essence.

3 Fold in the flour and cocoa mixture. Stir in the chocolate chips and hot water.

4 Spoon the mixture into six greased 175 ml (6 fl oz) moulds and place them upright in a large pan or deep-sided roasting tin with enough water to come half way up the basins. Cover with a tight-fitting lid and steam on the hob for about 45 minutes until risen and just firm.

5 Turn out and serve garnished with redcurrants and mint.

Bitter chocolate sauce

For a less bitter-tasting sauce, fold in a few spoonfuls of whipped cream to taste. Remember to use a good-quality plain chocolate.

SERVES 6

175 ml (6 fl oz) water
175 g (6 oz) plain chocolate, broken into pieces
2 tbsp cocoa powder
25 g (1 oz) butter

1 Heat the water in a pan and add the chocolate and cocoa. Stir until the chocolate has melted, without allowing the mixture to boil.

2 Add the butter, stir until melted, then serve.

CHOOSING THE FLOWERS
If the winter is drawing to a close, you may be lucky enough to pick up some early daffodils. For a fragrant touch, add a bunch of rosemary.

Chocolate shortbread with peaches

Nothing could be simpler than a butter shortbread, and our version combines this with luscious ripe peaches.

SERVES 6

50 g (2 oz) butter
50 g (2 oz) caster sugar
25 g (1 oz) cornflour
100 g (4 oz) plain flour
1 tbsp cocoa powder
3 ripe peaches, sliced
300 ml (10 fl oz) double cream, whipped
icing sugar, sifted

1 Preheat the oven to 180°C/350°F/gas mark 4.

2 Cream the butter and sugar. Sift the cornflour, flour and most of the cocoa together, then stir them into the butter and sugar to make a moderately firm but not stiff dough.

3 Use a light dusting of cocoa to stop the short-bread sticking and roll it out to a thickness of 5 mm ($\frac{1}{4}$ in).

4 Cut the shortbread into 12 rectangles and bake in the oven for 15–20 minutes. Leave to cool, then sandwich the peaches and cream between two pieces of shortbread and dust with icing sugar.

Some Like It Hot

A PINCH OF *spice makes everything warmer and tastier – and gives a new twist to ingredients more traditionally associated with Sunday lunch. Chilli, curry, peppers and limes combine in an easy menu with a fragrant Thai flavour.*

Menu for six

THAI FISH CAKES

—

SPICY COCONUT CHICKEN

STIR-FRIED CABBAGE

—

MANGO ICE CREAM

Thai fish cakes

Red Thai curry paste is available from most supermarkets, as is the fish sauce used in the dipping sauce. Alternatively, try Thai or oriental greengrocers. To save time, you could buy ready-made dipping sauces. The fish cake mixture can be made a day in advance and the fish cakes can be served either hot or at room temperature.

SERVES 6

700 g (1$\frac{1}{2}$ lb) skinless haddock fillet

1$\frac{1}{2}$ tbsp Thai fish sauce

1 egg

175 g (6 oz) cooked peeled prawns

5 spring onions, finely chopped

4 tbsp chopped fresh coriander

4 tsp red Thai curry paste

salt

a little flour

sunflower or corn oil

FOR THE HOT DIPPING SAUCE

2 tbsp Thai fish sauce

1 tbsp soy sauce, preferably Japanese

2 tsp sesame oil

1–2 tbsp lime juice

1 tsp brown sugar

a few slices of red chilli pepper

FOR THE SALAD

2 large carrots, coarsely grated

$\frac{1}{2}$ mooli (white radish), coarsely grated

2 tsp sesame seeds, toasted lambs' lettuce

1 Remove any bones from the fish, then cut the fillets into chunks and place in a food processor with the fish sauce and egg. Pulse until well mixed but not too smooth. Transfer to a bowl.

2 Process the prawns in the same way, then add to the fish with the spring onions, coriander and curry paste. Season with salt.

3 Shape the mixture into 18 fish cakes, patting them into shape and coating them lightly with flour.

4 Heat about 1 cm ($\frac{1}{2}$ in) of oil in a wok or frying pan. Fry the fish cakes for about 2 minutes on each side until golden brown and cooked through.

5 Mix the dipping sauce ingredients and place in a serving bowl.

6 Mix the salad ingredients and serve with the hot fish cakes and dipping sauce.

Spicy fish cakes served with salad and a hot dipping sauce.

Spicy coconut chicken

Try to prepare this a day in advance so that the flavours have time to develop. Leave it to cool thoroughly, then cover and chill until you are ready to reheat gently and serve. You will find coconut cream or milk and green Thai curry paste in all major supermarkets. Fresh lime leaves are available on their own or in packets with other Thai flavourings. If you cannot find fresh, you can use dried lime leaves instead. Serve the dish with boiled Thai jasmine rice.

SERVES 6

- 16–18 skinless, boneless chicken thigh pieces
- 3 tbsp corn oil
- salt and freshly ground black pepper
- 400 ml (14 fl oz) coconut cream or coconut milk
- 10–12 lime leaves, centre vein removed and snipped into strips
- 120 ml (4 fl oz) water
- 3 red, orange and yellow peppers, seeded and cut into strips
- 2–3 tbsp green Thai curry paste
- 8–10 large basil leaves, shredded

1 Trim off any fat from the chicken thighs and cut them into bite-sized pieces.

2 Heat 2 tbsp of the oil in a heavy-based, non-stick pan large enough to hold all the ingredients. Brown the chicken lightly in batches, removing it with a slotted spoon. When all the meat is browned, return it to the pan and season with salt and pepper.

3 Add the coconut cream or milk, lime leaves and water. Bring to the boil, then cover and simmer over a very low heat for 18–20 minutes until cooked through.

4 Meanwhile, heat the remaining oil in a non-stick pan. Add the peppers and cook over a medium heat, stirring frequently, for 4 minutes. Add the curry paste and cook for a further 2–3 minutes.

5 When the chicken is cooked, stir in the pepper strips with the curry paste and simmer for a further 5 minutes.

6 Lift out the chicken and pepper pieces, using a slotted spoon, and transfer to a warmed serving dish. Fast-boil the cooking juices until they thicken into a sauce. Season and stir in the basil.

Stir-fried cabbage

Stir-fried quickly over a fairly high heat, cabbage retains its freshness and colour and tastes deliciously tender but still crisp.

SERVES 6

3 tbsp sunflower or corn oil

1 red onion, very thinly sliced

3 garlic cloves, thinly sliced

900 g (2 lb) red cabbage, very finely shredded

salt and freshly ground black pepper

4 tbsp desiccated coconut

1 Heat 1 tbsp of the oil in a non-stick wok or frying pan. Add the onion and garlic and stir-fry over a medium heat for 1–2 minutes.

2 Add and heat the remaining oil, then add the shredded cabbage a little at a time. Season with salt and pepper and stir-fry for another 1–2 minutes. Add the desiccated coconut and stir-fry for another 1–2 minutes. Serve at once.

TABLE-TOP STYLE
The spicy colours of Thai food always look their best against cool, fresh blue china. For the finishing touch we added vases of marigolds, hebe, freesias and amaryllis.

Mango ice cream

If it is more convenient, you can turn out the ice cream on to the serving platter well in advance, then refreeze it. Remove the whole thing from the freezer and decorate shortly before serving.

SERVES 6

2 x 425 g (15 oz) tins of mango slices in syrup, drained

juice and grated zest of 1 lime

3 large eggs, separated

75 g (3 oz) caster sugar

300 ml (10 fl oz) double cream

TO DECORATE

3 ripe kiwi fruit, sliced

6–8 large strawberries

1 Line a 1 litre (1¾ pint) mould or loaf tin with clingfilm.

2 Blend the drained mango slices, lime juice and zest in a food processor to a smooth pulp. Set aside.

3 Place the egg yolks and the caster sugar in a bowl over a pan of barely simmering water and whisk for about 10 minutes until the mixture is very thick and the colour of pale straw. Fold the fruit purée into the beaten yolks.

4 Whip the cream until it stands in soft peaks, then fold into the mango and egg mixture.

5 Whisk the egg whites untill stiff, then fold them into the ice cream.

6 Spoon the ice cream mixture into the mould and smooth the surface. Freeze overnight or until required.

7 About 20 minutes before serving, remove the ice cream from the freezer. Dip the base and sides of the tin in warm water for a few seconds to help remove the ice cream from the tin. Turn out on to a chilled serving platter and peel away the clingfilm.

8 Arrange the kiwi slices around the base of the ice cream. Leaving the leaves intact, slice the strawberries from tip to base about three-quarters of the way down. Fan out the strawberry slices and arrange on top of the ice cream. Chill until ready to serve.

Opposite: *Rich and smooth mango ice cream looks impressive made in a decorative shape and dressed with colourful fruit.*

Weekend Favourites

THESE RECIPES *are ideal for blustery weekends and late-season breaks. Cheesy bakes and pan-fried fish are deliciously warming barbecue ideas make the most of sunnier days, and an easy fruit cake is the perfect snack for any time of day.*

Our speedy version of the classic French cassoulet not only tastes good but saves on washing up.

Quick country cassoulet

This makes a delicious and substantial lunch and comes in its own 'container' of crusty white bread.

SERVES 4

½ red onion, chopped
75 g (3 oz) streaky bacon, diced
350 g (12 oz) smoked pork sausages, sliced or diced
1 large garlic clove, crushed
a pinch of chilli powder
50 g (2 oz) stoned black olives, quartered
400 g (14 oz) tin of peeled, chopped tomatoes
85 ml (3 fl oz) water
1 large cob loaf
2 tbsp olive oil
400 g (4 oz) tin of kidney beans, rinsed and drained
150 g (5 oz) green beans, cooked and roughly chopped
150 g (5 oz) Mozzarella cheese, diced

1 Preheat the oven to 190°C/375°F/gas mark 5.

2 Cook the onion and bacon over a medium heat until the onion is soft and translucent. Add the sausage, garlic, chilli, olives, tomatoes and water. Bring to the boil, then simmer gently for 10 minutes.

3 Meanwhile, cut a shallow lid from the loaf of bread. Scoop out the inside of the loaf until little more than the crust remains. Brush the inside with olive oil and wrap with foil. Place the loaf in the oven and heat through for about 15 minutes.

4 Add the kidney beans and green beans to the pan and heat through. Finally stir in the Mozzarella. Spoon the mixture into the loaf and replace the lid.

5 Serve the cassoulet straight from the bread container, breaking off pieces of bread for your guests as you serve.

Pork and aubergine bake

The bake can be prepared in advance up to the point where the white sauce is poured over it and chilled overnight, ready to complete.

SERVES 4

3 tbsp olive oil

450 g (1 lb) lean minced pork

1 onion, finely chopped

1 garlic clove, crushed

1 tsp allspice

1 tsp ground coriander

200 g (7 oz) tin of peeled, chopped tomatoes

1 tbsp tomato purée

a pinch of dried thyme

salt and freshly ground black pepper

300 g (10 oz) courgettes, thinly sliced

400 g (14 oz) aubergines, thinly sliced

olive oil

300 ml (10 fl oz) of white sauce packet mix

1 large egg, beaten

40 g (1½ oz) Cheddar cheese, grated

1 Preheat the oven to 190°C/375°F/gas mark 5.

2 Heat 1 tbsp of the oil in a heavy-based pan. Add the pork and brown it lightly, breaking the meat up with a wooden spoon as it cooks.

3 Add the onion and garlic and cook until the onion is soft and translucent.

4 Add the spices, tomatoes, tomato purée and thyme and season to taste. Bring to the boil, then cover and simmer gently for 10 minutes.

5 Place the courgettes and aubergines on a lightly greased roasting tray, brush with oil and roast for 10 minutes. Turn the vegetables over and brush with a little more oil, then return to the oven for a further 10 minutes until tender. Reduce the oven temperature to 180°C/ 350°F/ gas mark 4.

6 Cover the bottom of a gratin dish with about one-third of the pork mixture. Cover with half the aubergine slices. Add another layer of pork followed by a layer of courgettes. Add the final layer of pork and top with the remaining aubergines.

7 Make the white sauce as directed on the packet, then leave to cool slightly. Whisk in the beaten egg and stir in the cheese. Spoon the sauce over the top and bake

This tasty pork and aubergine dish makes a delicious meal that requires only a little preparation – just what's needed after a day out in the fresh air.

in the oven for about 35–40 minutes until the top is crisp and golden brown.

INSTANT WINTER BARBECUES

Even on winter days it is often warm enough to make use of a portable barbecue on a day out or in the garden – and it will make a pleasantly surprising change for your guests.

MARINATED CHICKEN DRUMSTICKS

Before you leave home, or an hour or so before you cook, place some chicken drumsticks in large plastic food bags and add a ready-made marinade of your choice. Knot the top of the bag to seal it and the chicken will be ready to barbecue as soon as you arrive.

BARBECUED SWEET POTATOES

Thickly sliced sweet potatoes are a tasty accompaniment. Simply brush with a little oil and season with salt and pepper. Place around the drumsticks and cook until tender.

BARBECUED FRUIT SKEWERS

Wedges of fruit, such as apples, pears and plums, are ideal for a quick dessert. Don't peel them – the skin will hold the wedges together – just thread on to metal skewers. Blend a little clear honey, lemon juice and oil (use a flavourless one such as sunflower or corn oil). Brush over the fruit and cook on the barbecue until golden, turning the skewers occasionally and brushing with the honey mixture. Serve with ice cream.

Crispy lemon mackerel

Delicious cooked indoors or out. Ask your fishmonger to fillet some mackerel for you to save some work.

SERVES 4

4 large mackerel fillets
freshly ground black pepper
2 tbsp olive oil
salt
2 lemons, cut into wedges

TO SERVE

new potatoes
sugar snap peas

1 Wash the fillets and dry thoroughly on kitchen paper. Season with black pepper.

2 Heat a little oil in a heavy non-stick pan. When the oil is sizzling, add the fillets one at a time, skin-side down. When crisp and golden, turn and cook on the other side. Remove the fillets from the pan, sprinkle with crushed sea salt and keep warm.

3 In the same pan, quickly fry some lemon wedges. Serve the fish with the lemon wedges, new potatoes, boiled in their skins, and a bowl of steamed sugar snap peas.

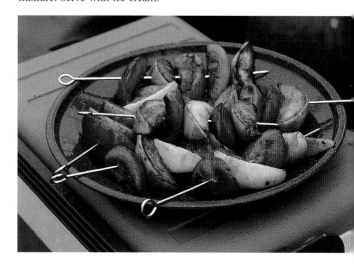

Easy fruit cake

The great advantage of fruit cake is that it stores well in a airtight container, so it's an ideal winter snack.

CUTS INTO 10
  SLICES

200 g (7 oz) soft
  margarine
150 g (5 oz) light
  soft brown sugar
5 eggs, separated
200 g (7 oz) plain flour
90 g (3½ oz) currants
15–20 blanched almonds,
  halved lengthways

1 Preheat the oven to 180°C/350°F/gas mark 4. Line the base of an 18 cm (7 in) cake tin with parchment paper. Grease thoroughly and set aside.

2 Using an electric whisk, beat the margarine and sugar until light and fluffy. Beat in the egg yolks one at a time until well blended.

3 Mix the flour and currants. Stir gently but thoroughly into the mixture.

4 Clean the whisk well – any grease left on the whisk will stop the egg whites from stiffening. Beat the egg whites until they form soft peaks. Fold about one-third of the beaten whites into the batter to slacken the mixture. Carefully fold in the remaining egg whites.

5 Spoon the batter into the prepared tin and bake in the oven for 5 minutes. Remove the tin from the oven and quickly arrange the almonds in a pattern on the surface of the cake.

6 Return to the oven for a further 50–55 minutes until a skewer inserted in the centre comes out clean.

Traditional Sunday Lunch

ALL THE best British flavours are combined here for a traditional menu that no one can resist. Ideal for family get-togethers and leisurely Sundays, it's a real classic that deserves the best china.

Menu for ten

SIMPLE SMOKED SALMON PÂTÉ

SPICY CHEESE-TOPPED CRAB

—

ROAST BEEF WITH POTATOES AND PARSNIPS

MIXED GREEN BEANS IN BUTTER

BRAISED CELERY

CLASSIC YORKSHIRE PUDDINGS

RED WINE GRAVY

—

MADEIRA TRIFLE WITH ALMONDS AND RASPBERRIES

Simple smoked salmon pâté

Serve this tasty starter with crisp slices of toast.

SERVES 10

250 g (9 oz) smoked salmon slices, chopped

225 g (8 oz) curd or Ricotta cheese

4 tbsp lemon juice

85 ml (3 fl oz) double cream

freshly ground black pepper

4 tbsp snipped fresh chives

1 lemon, sliced

1 Purée 175 g (6 oz) of the salmon with the cheese, lemon juice, cream and pepper until fairly smooth.

2 Stir in 3 tbsp of the chives and the remaining salmon.

3 Place in shallow serving dish and garnish with the remaining chives and the lemon slices.

Spicy cheese-topped crab

This looks especially effective if you make it in scallop shells or attractive ramekin dishes. Serve it with triangles of freshly buttered brown bread.

SERVES 10

25 g (1 oz) butter
½ small onion, chopped
25 g (1 oz) plain flour
300 ml (10 fl oz) single cream
1 tbsp Dijon mustard
2–3 tbsp Worcestershire sauce
2 tsp anchovy essence
a good pinch of cayenne pepper
500 g (18 oz) fresh white and brown crab meat
75–100 g (3–4 oz) fresh white breadcrumbs
salt and freshly ground black pepper

FOR THE TOPPING

4 tbsp dried breadcrumbs
75 g (3 oz) strong Cheddar cheese, grated
1 tbsp finely chopped fresh parsley
1 lemon, cut into wedges

1 Preheat the oven to 190°C/375°F/gas mark 5.

2 Melt the butter and sauté the onion until soft. Stir in the flour and cook for 1 minute, then remove from the heat.

3 Heat the cream to simmering point, then gradually stir into the onion mixture. Bring to the boil, stirring constantly, then simmer for a few minutes.

4 Stir in the remaining ingredients and season with salt and pepper.

5 Lightly grease ten scallop shells or ramekin dishes and divide the crab mixture between them. Mix the breadcrumbs and cheese and sprinkle over the top. Bake in the oven for 15–20 minutes until golden. Serve garnished with parsley and lemon wedges.

The crab starter can be prepared in advance then finished with the topping and baked when you are ready.

Roast beef with potatoes and parsnips

Beef is still perfect for special lunches. Choose a joint that's dark red with creamy white fat and fine marbling. If you buy beef off the bone, it will weigh slightly less; simply calculate your cooking time accordingly. Always allow roast meat to rest in a warm place for at least 15 minutes to make it easier to carve and give you time to finish the accompaniments.

SERVES 10

2 tbsp plain flour
1 tbsp mustard powder
salt and freshly ground black pepper
3.5 kg (8 lb) rib of beef
1.6 kg (3½ lb) potatoes, cut into even-sized chunks
1.5 kg (3 lb) parsnips, cut into pieces
10 medium onions, quartered

1 Preheat the oven to 190°C/375°F/gas mark 5. Calculate the roasting time of your joint based on 15 minutes per 450 g (lb) for medium. If you prefer it rarer, reduce the total cooking time by 15 minutes. For well-done meat, roast for 20 minutes per 450 g (lb) plus another 15 minutes.

2 Blend the flour and mustard and season with salt and pepper. Rub the mixture into the joint.

3 Place the joint, fat-side up, in a roasting tray and roast in the oven for the time calculated, basting occasionally.

4 Meanwhile, parboil the potatoes and parsnips in lightly salted boiling water for 5 minutes. Drain.

5 About 1¼ hours before the meat is cooked, spoon most of the fat from the roasting tray and reserve. Place the onions around the meat and return it to the oven. Baste occasionally until the onions are golden brown.

6 Pour some of the reserved fat into a large roasting tray so that it is about 5 mm (¼ in) deep. Place in the oven above the roast until sizzling. Add the potatoes and parsnips and roast until crisp and golden, basting occasionally.

7 When the meat is ready, lift it out of the roasting tray with the onions. Wrap in a double layer of foil and leave to rest in a warm place while you cook the Yorkshire pudding and gravy (see opposite).

Mixed green beans in butter

A richly coloured dish which adds a wonderful contrast to the main course. Make sure you don't overcook the beans – keep them crisp and they will retain not only their flavour but also their sharp colour.

SERVES 10

400 g (14 oz) broad beans
400 g (14 oz) runner beans
400 g (14 oz) French beans
75 g (3 oz) butter

1 Prepare the broad beans by popping them out of their skins. Top and tail the runner beans, remove the stringy side pieces and slice the beans thinly. Top and tail the French beans.

2 Cook the beans separately in lightly salted boiling water until just tender but still crisp to the bite. Drain well.

3 Toss the beans with butter and spoon into a warmed serving dish.

Braised celery

A much underrated vegetable, celery should not be confined to salads and lunch boxes. Cooked in stock and butter, it makes a lovely accompaniment to roast beef.

SERVES 10

3 celery hearts, trimmed
75 g (3 oz) butter
300 ml (10 fl oz) chicken stock
freshly ground black pepper

1 Cut the celery hearts into 7.5 cm (3 in) lengths. Blanch in lightly salted boiling water for 4–5 minutes, then drain well.

2 Melt the butter in a heavy-based, lidded pan, add the celery and toss in the butter.

3 Add the stock and season with pepper.

4 Cover and simmer over a very low heat for 50–60 minutes until the celery is very tender, adding a little more water if required.

Red wine gravy

Adding a little wine to your gravy gives it a rich flavour and added colour.

SERVES 10

4 tbsp plain flour
150 ml (5 fl oz) red wine
900 ml (1½ pints) vegetable stock

1 Once the meat is cooked, pour off any excess fat from the roasting tray. Stir in the flour, scraping the sediment from the bottom of the tray. Mix well and cook briefly over low heat, stirring continuously.

2 Remove from the heat and gradually stir in the wine, then the stock. Bring to the boil, then simmer for 4–5 minutes. Strain.

Classic Yorkshire puddings

This recipe gives great results every time.

SERVES 10

Make the batter while the meat is roasting and leave it to stand for 30 minutes before using.

2 large eggs
100 g (4 oz) plain flour, sifted
300 ml (10 fl oz) full-fat milk
a pinch of salt

1 Whisk all the ingredients together to make a smooth batter.

2 Spoon a little beef fat into a bun tray or Yorkshire pudding tins.

3 While the beef is resting, increase the oven temperature to 230°C/450°F/gas mark 8.

4 Heat the fat until sizzling hot, then divide the batter between the hollows.

5 Bake for 15–20 minutes until puffed and golden.

Madeira trifle with almonds and raspberries

This is best prepared a day in advance to allow the flavours to develop fully.

SERVES 10

350 g (12 oz) Madeira cake
3 tbsp seedless raspberry jam
6 tbsp Madeira or Marsala
450 g (1 lb) fresh or frozen raspberries
3 tbsp caster sugar
600 ml (1 pint) ready-made custard
350 ml (12 fl oz) double cream
3 tbsp icing sugar, sifted
40 g (1½ oz) flaked almonds, toasted

1 Cut the cake into 1 cm (½ in) slices. Spread with raspberry jam and use to line the base and half way up the sides of a large, shallow glass bowl.

2 Pour over the Madeira or Marsala.

3 Reserve a few of the raspberries for decoration, then mix the rest with the caster sugar. Leave to stand for a few minutes, stir well, then spoon over the cake.

4 Cover with custard, cover and chill for at least 3–4 hours.

5 Before serving, whip the cream and 2 tbsp of the icing sugar until it stands in soft peaks. Swirl over the trifle and decorate with raspberries, almonds and a dusting of icing sugar.

Special

Occasions

EVERYONE HAS their own way of celebrating: old family traditions, memories shared with old friends – or just a spontaneous party for a one-off event. But sometimes it's nice to be able to pick up a recipe and know that this is the one that will suit the occasion, without having to think about it. All these recipes are perfect standbys for times when you really don't want things to go wrong.

Celebration Spread

THIS MENU is best for summer, where eating alfresco will make the most of the season's flavours and colours. There's a mix of starters to whet your guests' appetites, then a splendid salmon en croûte and, to finish, a celebratory pyramid of fresh cream profiteroles served with chocolate sauce and raspberries.

Menu for ten

PESTO TOMATOES

MANGO PRAWNS

CRISPY CHICKEN

—

SALMON EN CROUTE
WITH HOLLANDAISE SAUCE

—

PROFITEROLE PYRAMID

Pesto tomatoes

This essentially Italian-style recipe makes a refreshing starter for any meal.

MAKES 20

10 small, firm, ripe red tomatoes (not cherry ones)

1 ball of Mozzarella cheese, diced

1 medium-sized avocado, peeled, stoned and diced

1 heaped tbsp pesto

salt and freshly ground black pepper

1 Halve the tomatoes cross-ways, scoop out the seeds and place the tomato halves upside-down on kitchen paper to drain off the juices.

2 Mix the Mozzarella, avocado and pesto, then season.

3 Pile the filling into the tomatoes and serve.

Mango prawns

Raw tiger prawns are available either fresh or frozen. They are perfect if just cooked until they turn pink; don't overcook them or they will lose their delicate flavour and texture.

MAKES 20

20 medium-sized, raw tiger prawns
1 garlic clove, crushed
1 tbsp soy sauce
3 tbsp olive oil
juice of 1 lime
a pinch of crushed dried red chilli peppers
salt and freshly ground black pepper
1 large ripe, firm mango

1 Carefully remove the heads and tails from the prawns. Rinse well in cold water and dry on kitchen paper.

2 Blend the garlic, soy sauce, 2 tbsp of the olive oil, the lime juice and chillies and season to taste. Add the prawns and toss well. Marinate for 30 minutes, then drain well.

3 Heat the remaining oil over a high heat in a non-stick pan and fry the prawns until they turn pink. Leave to cool.

4 Peel and slice the mango, then cut into chunks. Thread the prawns on to cocktail sticks with a piece of mango at each end.

Crispy chicken

Buy ready-to-cook, marinated chicken wings, trim off and discard the very end bits of the wings (the pinions) and cut the wings in half. Grill until cooked through, well browned and crisp, turning several times. Serve the chicken hot or cold.

Salmon en croûte

This can be prepared the night before so that it just needs to be brushed with egg and baked on the day. Cover and keep chilled until ready to complete.

SERVES 10–12

1 x 2 kg (4$\frac{1}{2}$ lb) gutted salmon

salt and freshly ground black pepper

500 g (18 oz) puff pastry

1 egg, beaten

1 olive, sliced

a juniper berry or peppercorn

FOR THE STUFFING

40 g (1$\frac{1}{2}$ oz) fresh white breadcrumbs

40 g (1$\frac{1}{2}$ oz) butter

grated zest of $\frac{1}{2}$ lemon

3 tbsp finely chopped fresh parsley

1 Ask your fishmonger to skin and fillet the salmon, removing the head. Remove any remaining bones using tweezers. Wipe the fillets on kitchen paper. Trim the head end of the fillets to a slightly pointed shape. Season and set aside.

2 Mix together the stuffing ingredients.

3 From greaseproof paper, cut a fish-shaped template slightly longer and wider than the fish, adding a simple tail shape at one end. Roll out just over one-third of the pastry and cut out a fish shape, using the template.

4 Place the pastry on a dampened non-stick baking sheet with no sides and leave to rest for 30 minutes in the fridge.

5 Preheat the oven to 230°C/450°F/gas mark 8.

6 Prick the pastry all over, then bake in the oven for 10 minutes. Turn it over and

bake for a further 10 minutes. Leave until cold.

7 Place one of the fish fillets on top of the cooked pastry. Arrange the stuffing evenly over the surface. Place a second fillet on top, fitting the back on the top fillet underneath to get as even a surface as possible.

8 Roll out the remaining pastry into a rectangle large enough to cover the entire fish, leaving enough pastry to tuck under the edges of the cooked pastry base. Carefully lift the pastry on to the fish and trim off excess pastry. Brush the edges with a little beaten egg and tuck them under the base.

9 Using a plain icing nozzle or a small biscuit cutter, make scale shapes on the fish from the tail up to the head. Pierce the pastry in a few places to allow steam to escape. Make fins, gills and an eye from leftover pastry, and attach with a little beaten egg. Make fin and tail patterns with the back of a knife and place a slice of olive, a juniper berry or a peppercorn in the centre of the eye.

10 Brush the pastry with beaten egg and cook in the oven for 15 minutes. Reduce the oven temperature to 160°C/325°F/gas mark 3 and bake for a further

Served buffet-style, the main course consists of salmon in pastry with Hollandaise sauce and steamed vegetables.

25–30 minutes. The fish is cooked when a thin skewer can easily be pushed through.

11 Leave to rest for a few minutes, then run a very sharp, thin-bladed knife under the fish to loosen it from the tray. Use fish slices or palette knives to transfer it to a serving platter.

12 Serve surrounded by steamed, buttered baby vegetables and accompanied by small new potatoes cooked with dill.

Profiterole pyramid

Since the profiteroles are so tiny, you will need to keep an eye on the cooking time. They can be baked a day or two in advance, then stored in an airtight container in a cool place and filled on the day. They can also be frozen – thaw for at least an hour before filling.

MAKES ABOUT 50 TINY PROFITEROLES

100 g (4 oz) butter
300 ml (10 fl oz) water
150 g (5 oz) plain flour
4 eggs, beaten
icing sugar, sifted

FOR THE FILLING

350 g (12 oz) white chocolate drops or diced white chocolate
750 ml ($1\frac{1}{4}$ pints) crème fraîche

FOR THE CHOCOLATE SAUCE

225 g (8 oz) caster sugar
300 ml (10 fl oz) water
100 g (4 oz) cocoa powder, sifted
1 tbsp instant coffee

1 Preheat the oven to 230°C/450°F/gas mark 8.

2 For the profiteroles, place the butter and water in a heavy-based pan. Heat gently until the butter melts, then increase the heat and bring to the boil.

3 Remove from the heat and quickly add the flour. Beat thoroughly with a wooden spoon until the mixture forms a ball. Allow to cool a little.

4 Beat in the eggs, a little at a time, and continue beating until the mixture is smooth and shiny.

5 Use a plain 1 cm ($\frac{1}{2}$ in) nozzle to pipe balls of the mixture about the size of a large radish and 4 cm ($1\frac{1}{2}$ in) apart on to dampened baking sheets.

6 Bake in the oven for 10 minutes, then reduce the oven temperature to 190°C/375°F/gas mark 5 and bake for a further 18–20 minutes. Test a couple of profiteroles first – they should be well-risen, golden brown and cooked through but still a little moist inside. Leave to cool on a rack and use scissors to snip a hole in the top of each one, allowing steam to escape.

7 For the filling, melt the white chocolate in a heatproof bowl over a pan of barely simmering water, stirring occasionally. Remove from the heat and cool a little. Gradually add the crème fraîche and beat until smooth. Leave until cold.

8 Pipe the filling into the cold profiteroles and pile them on to a serving plate.

9 To make the sauce, heat the sugar and water gently in a pan until the sugar dissolves. Bring to the boil and fast boil for 2 minutes.

10 Off the heat, whisk in the cocoa and coffee until smooth. Set aside to cool, stirring occasionally.

11 Spoon a little sauce over the profiteroles, letting it run down the sides, then dust with icing sugar. Serve the rest of the sauce separately.

Easy Hollandaise sauce

Hollandaise sauce is served warm. It can't be reheated, but this version takes only a couple of minutes to prepare, so make it just as the rest of the meal is ready to serve. You can keep the sauce warm for a short while by standing the serving bowl in a pan of warm water.

SERVES 10

6 egg yolks
50 ml (2 fl oz) tarragon vinegar
salt and a generous pinch of cayenne pepper
200 g (7 oz) butter

1 Briefly blend the egg yolks, tarragon vinegar, salt and cayenne pepper in a food processor.

2 Melt the butter, then heat until bubbling hot.

3 Turn the processor to maximum speed and gradually pour in the melted butter. Process briefly until the sauce is thick and fluffy.

4 Transfer to a warm serving jug or bowl and serve at once.

The Children's Party

THEY'RE NOTORIOUSLY *hard to please, but this colourful menu, full of all their favourite flavours, is guaranteed to keep kids happy. It's ideal for birthday brunches and other special occasions.*

Clockwise from right: French toast smiles, good morning specials, baby bagels, honey and sesame seed sausages, bonfire sandwiches.

Menu for six

FRENCH TOAST SMILES

GOOD MORNING SPECIALS

BABY BAGELS

HONEY AND SESAME SEED SAUSAGES

BONFIRE SANDWICHES

—

DOUBLE CHOCOLATE MINI MUFFINS

MINI RING DOUGHNUTS

ST CLEMENT'S JELLIES

—

BANANA MILKSHAKE

74

French toast smiles

A fun version of eggy bread with faces made of tomato ketchup. You can change it into an adult version by adding wholegrain mustard and mixed herbs to any leftover egg.

SERVE 1–2 PER CHILD

sliced white bread
eggs, beaten
oil for frying
cherry tomatoes, halved
tomato ketchup
mushrooms (optional)

1 Cut the bread into rounds using a large pastry cutter or jar lid. Cut out mouths with a knife.

2 Dip the bread into beaten egg and fry each side for a few seconds in medium hot oil. Drain well on kitchen paper, then add cherry tomato halves for the eyes and tomato ketchup for the noses. You can even add a few chopped and fried mushrooms for hair.

Good morning specials

Combine breakfast favourites for these neat savoury tartlets. The tartlet cases, scrambled egg and tomato halves can all be prepared a day in advance and then warmed up before serving.

SERVE 2–3 PER CHILD

thinly sliced brown bread
melted butter
baked beans
cherry tomatoes, halved and lightly grilled
scrambled eggs

1 Preheat the oven to 180°C/350°F/gas mark 4.

2 Remove the crusts from the bread and roll the bread out slightly. Cut out small bread rounds, dip into melted butter and press into a mini muffin tin, butter-side down.

3 Cook in the oven for about 10 minutes until crisp, then fill the tartlets with a spoonful of baked beans, lightly grilled cherry tomato halves and scrambled eggs.

SETTING THE SCENE

Children and china don't mix, but you can still create a wonderful dressed-up party table using paper plates – which also cuts down the clearing-up time to a minimum. We chose a fun combination of spots and stripes in blues and golds and added more dressy touches by decorating the table with colourful ribbons and having plenty of pale pink balloons. Try to get some fun plastic tumblers with built-in straws. If you can't get a plastic-coated tablecloth, try using a bold, plain cotton or gingham check fabric – but don't forget to protect your table against spills!

Baby bagels

Most children adore smoked salmon and, with their slightly sweet taste and their soft chewy texture, bagels are really easy to eat. Look out for the offcuts of smoked salmon as these are much cheaper than whole fillets. If you don't want to use smoked salmon pieces, you can now buy cream cheese in a tasty salmon and dill flavour.

SERVE 1–2 PER CHILD

1 Slice the bagels in half, spread with cream cheese and scatter sparingly with shredded smoked salmon.

2 Cut the bagels into quarters for the children and serve adults whole ones seasoned with a good grinding of black pepper and a squeeze of fresh lemon juice.

Honey and sesame seed sausages

Use small cocktail-style sausages as they're perfect for smaller fingers. Avoid sausages flavoured with a lot of herbs and spices.

SERVE 4–6 PER CHILD

cocktail sausages
runny honey
sesame seeds

1 Preheat the oven to 180°C/350°F/gas mark 4.

2 Cook the sausages in the oven for 15–20 minutes with a few tablespoons of runny honey and a splash of water. Sprinkle with sesame seeds once cooked and allow to cool before serving.

Bonfire sandwiches make a popular treat. For fun sandwiches, pair up slices of wholemeal and white bread, or cut them into circles with a pastry cutter.

Bonfire sandwiches

A delicious combination of crispy bacon and fruit jam on a bed of mixed pepper 'flames'.

SERVE 2–3 PER CHILD

bacon rashers

sliced white bread, crusts removed

apricot jam

red and yellow peppers, seeded and cut into strips

1 Fry the bacon until very crisp, then make the sandwiches by combining chipped bacon pieces and thinly spread apricot jam.

2 Cut into triangles and pile on a plate with slices of red and yellow pepper to create a flame effect.

Double chocolate mini muffins

Chocolate is a safe bet for any children's party as they all seem to love it. Mini muffins are ideal for small children, but you can make the cakes in full-size muffin tins or cases and bake them for about 15 minutes.

MAKES 24

150 g (5 oz) plain flour

1 tsp baking powder

25 g (1 oz) cocoa powder

2 tbsp caster sugar

50 g (2 oz) chocolate chips

1 egg

175 ml (6 fl oz) milk

50 g (2 oz) butter, melted

1 Preheat the oven to 200°C/400°F/gas mark 6.

2 Sift together the flour, baking powder and cocoa, then stir in the sugar and chocolate chips.

3 Beat together the egg and milk and pour on to the flour and chocolate mixture. Add the melted butter and stir until the dry ingredients are just combined; the mixture will still be lumpy but do not overmix.

4 Spoon into muffin cases or well-greased mini muffin tins and bake in the oven for 10 minutes.

Mini ring doughnuts

Experiment with the first few doughnuts in order to get the right size and shape. They cook very quickly, so don't let your attention wander while you are frying.

MAKES 24

350 g (12 oz) self-raising flour

$\frac{1}{2}$ tsp ground cinnamon

a pinch of salt

100 g (4 oz) butter

100 g (4 oz) caster sugar plus extra for sprinkling

150 ml (5 fl oz) milk

1 egg

oil for deep-frying

1 Sift together the flour, cinnamon and salt. Rub in the butter, then add the sugar and mix to a soft dough with the milk and egg. Knead on a floured board until smooth.

2 Roll the dough in your hand to form a sausage. Break into roughly 15 cm (6 in) sections and press the two ends of each one together to form a ring.

3 Heat the oil and fry the doughnuts for 1–2 minutes until golden. Drain on kitchen paper, then sprinkle with caster sugar.

St Clement's jellies

Every party has to have jellies, but these are jellies with a difference — served in their own fruit shells. You can use the fruit flesh for another recipe.

SERVES 6–8

2 small oranges

2 limes

2 lemons

250 ml (8 fl oz) apple and blackcurrant juice

250 ml (8 fl oz) orange juice

4 tsp powdered gelatine

1 Halve the fruit, cutting the lemons and limes lengthways so they sit firmly, and carefully scrape away the flesh to leave you with cups. Use the fruit in another recipe.

2 Heat a little apple and blackcurrant juice, sprinkle over 2 tsp of the gelatine and stir until dissolved. You may need to reheat the juice slightly but don't let it boil. Stir in the remaining apple and blackcurrant juice. Repeat the jelly-making process with the orange juice.

3 Pour the jelly into the fruit halves, making sure that they are full to the top. Chill until set, then cut into quarters to serve.

Banana milkshake

This makes a healthy alternative to bottles of pop. If they're determined to have fizz, mix fruit cordial wth soda water.

SERVES 6

1 litre (1 $\frac{3}{4}$ pints) cold semi-skimmed milk

2 ripe bananas, chopped

6 scoops of vanilla ice cream

1 Put the milk and bananas into a liquidizer and blend until frothy.

2 Serve in tall glasses with a colourful straw and a generous scoop of ice cream.

A Classic English Tea

TEATIME ISN'T taken seriously these days — but for some occasions it's simply the nicest way to celebrate. We've mixed classic savouries with traditional treats for an irresistible spread that has a distinctive touch of old-fashioned charm.

Tea with a twist

Try these interesting variations on the traditional cup of tea. Once they have infused, strain and serve with a slice of lemon, if liked.

Ginger and lemon tea

Infuse 6 slices of peeled ginger root and 6 slices of lemon in 600 ml (1 pint) of boiling water for 5 minutes.

Orange and cardamom tea

Infuse 8 slices of orange, 4 cardamom seeds crushed with the back of your hand and 2 tsp of clear honey in 600 ml (1 pint) of boiling water for 5–8 minutes.

Cinnamon and allspice tea

Infuse 1 tsp of tea leaves, a cinnamon stick and 3 allspice berries in 600 ml (1 pint) of boiling water for 3–5 minutes. Add lemon juice and sugar to taste and serve.

SETTING THE SCENE
Classic blue and white china makes the perfect table setting for teatime and conjures up exactly the right sense of tradition. To create a less formal feel, mix and match different patterns including a few older pieces from the kitchen. If you're preparing herbal teas or infusions, try serving them in tea glasses.

Caraway seed cake

This cake tastes delicious served when it is still slightly warm.

SERVES 6

225 g (8 oz) butter
225 g (8 oz) caster sugar
4 large eggs
225 g (8 oz) plain flour
2 tsp caraway seeds
1 tsp vanilla essence

1 Preheat the oven to 180°C/350°F/gas mark 4. Grease a 20 cm (8 in) cake tin and line with baking parchment.

2 Cream the butter and sugar until very light and fluffy. Beat in the eggs one at a time with 1 tbsp of flour. Stir in the caraway seeds and vanilla essence. With a large metal spoon, fold in the remaining flour and transfer to the cake tin, smoothing the top.

3 Bake in the oven for 1 hour or until a wooden skewer inserted in the centre comes out clean. Allow to cool slightly before turning out on to a wire rack.

Clockwise from top: Earl Grey tea loaf, brandy bakewell tart, Yorkshire lemon tarts, quick and easy poppy seed scones.

Welsh rarebit crumpet toasties

Crumpet fingers make this easier to serve, but you can use the round variety if you prefer.

SERVES 6

40 g (1 $\frac{1}{2}$ oz) cold butter, grated
100 g (4 oz) mature Cheddar or Cheshire cheese, grated
1 large egg, lightly beaten
1 $\frac{1}{2}$ tsp Dijon mustard
1 $\frac{1}{2}$ tsp black mustard seeds
a dash of Worcestershire sauce
6 finger crumpets
a pinch of cayenne pepper

1 Mix the butter, cheese, egg, mustard and mustard seeds. Add a good dash of Worcestershire sauce.

2 Toast the underside of the crumpet fingers, then turn them over and spread the cheese mixture equally on top. Sprinkle with cayenne pepper.

3 Place under the grill until brown and bubbling. Serve immediately.

Brandy bakewell tart

The addition of the brandy gives this traditional favourite an extra boost. If you prefer to leave out the brandy, moisten the mixture instead with a little milk.

SERVES 6

225 g (8 oz) shortcrust pastry
3 tbsp red fruit jam
100 g (4 oz) butter
100 g (4 oz) caster sugar
2 tbsp brandy
2 eggs, lightly beaten
100 g (4 oz) ground almonds
25 g (1 oz) plain flour
2 tbsp flaked almonds

TO SERVE

double cream, whipped or single cream

1 Preheat the oven to 200°C/400°F/gas mark 6.

2 Roll out the pastry and use to line a greased 18 cm (7 in) flan case. Spread the pastry with the jam.

3 Cream the butter and sugar until pale and fluffy. Stir in all the remaining ingredients except the flaked almonds and spread the mixture over the jam.

4 Sprinkle on the flaked almonds and, if you have any remaining pastry, make a criss-cross pattern on top of the tarts.

5 Cook in the oven for 25–30 minutes. Serve warm or cold with cream.

Earl Grey tea loaf

This loaf is an excellent way to use up dried fruit and slightly stale bran cereals, while the Earl Grey tea adds moistness and a subtle flavour to the mixture.

SERVES 6

225 g (8 oz) dried fruit

100 g (4 oz) bran breakfast cereal

300 ml (10 fl oz) strong Earl Grey tea

50 g (2 oz) sugar

50 g (2 oz) butter, melted

2 large eggs, lightly beaten

100 g (4 oz) self-raising flour

1 Preheat the oven to 180°C/350°F/gas mark 4.

2 Mix the fruit and cereal. Pour on the tea and leave to stand for 10 minutes.

3 Stir in all the other ingredients and spoon into a well-greased 900 g (2 lb) loaf tin. Bake in the oven for 35–40 minutes. Allow to cool before turning out and serve sliced with a generous spread of butter.

Quick and easy poppy seed scones

The secret of good scones is to work the dough quickly and very lightly and then eat the finished scones within about an hour of cooking. Serve them with plenty of good-quality jam and thick cream or clotted cream.

MAKES 8–10

225 g (8 oz) self-raising flour

½ tsp salt

25–50 g (1–2 oz) butter

4 tbsp soured cream or crème fraîche

4 tbsp milk

poppy seeds

ground cinnamon

caster sugar

1 Preheat the oven to 230°C/450°F/gas mark 8.

2 Sift the flour and salt into a bowl, then rub in the butter. Mix in the cream or crème fraîche and enough of the milk to make a soft dough. Knead very lightly until smooth.

3 Roll out to about 1 cm (½ in) thick and cut into 8–10 rounds. Brush with the remaining milk, sprinkle with poppy seeds, cinnamon and sugar and bake in the oven for 6–10 minutes.

Yorkshire lemon tarts

If you can't find curd cheese, use cream cheese instead. If you are really short of time, replace the lemons and egg yolks with 6 tbsp of good-quality lemon curd.

MAKES 12 SMALL TARTS

250 g (9 oz) ready-rolled shortcrust pastry
juice and grated zest of 2 large lemons
225 g (8 oz) curd cheese
50 g (2 oz) caster sugar
2 eggs, separated

1. Preheat the oven to 180°C/350°F/gas mark 4.

2. Line a 12–hole Yorkshire pudding tray with circles of the pastry and prick with a fork.

3. Mix the lemon zest and juice, curd cheese, sugar and egg yolks.

4. Whisk the egg whites until stiff, then fold into the cheese mixture.

5. Spoon the mixture into the pastry cases and bake in the oven for 20–25 minutes or until the tops are just turning brown and the filling is set.

Nutty chocolate crunch cake

Unbelievably simple and deliciously more-ish. If you want to make this even more luxurious, add some fresh cherries and a little extra grated coconut

SERVES 6

450 g (1 lb) plain or milk chocolate
170 g (6 oz) digestive biscuits, crushed
1 tbsp desiccated coconut
1 tbsp chopped nuts
2 tbsp dried cherries

1. Melt the chocolate in a heatproof bowl over a pan of barely simmering water. Stir in all the other ingredients. Press into a shallow dish lined with baking parchment.

2. Leave in the fridge for 1 hour until hard. Break into pieces and serve.

FINISHING TOUCHES
Make the most of whatever burst of colour you can find in the garden borders or the shops. We chose tulips in white and pale pink and added a dash of stronger colour with yellow and red variegated varieties.

Easter Feasts

SPRING FLAVOURS *are always deliciously tempting. Pick and mix these recipes to create your own celebration menu.*

Asparagus bundles

If you have an asparagus steamer, do use it as it is designed to keep the vegetables upright so that the delicate tips are not overcooked.

SERVES 6

30 asparagus spears
1 small leek, cut into strips and blanched
18 bacon rashers, cut into strips
a selection of salad leaves
2 tbsp pesto
juice of 2 lemons
ciabatta

1 Trim the asparagus and bind in bundles of 5–6 with strips of blanched leek.

Steam or boil until tender, then drain the asparagus thoroughly.

2 Meanwhile, grill the bacon strips until crisp.

3 Arrange a bed of salad leaves on a serving plate, top with the asparagus and sprinkle with bacon.

4 Mix the pesto and lemon juice, drizzle over the asparagus and serve with slices of ciabatta.

Tomato nests

The filling and tomatoes can be prepared in advance, but avoid chilling them or the rice will take on a very starchy flavour.

SERVES 6

12 beefsteak tomatoes
150 g (5 oz) long-grain rice
salt
2 tbsp olive oil
1 onion, chopped
2 garlic cloves, chopped
1 small red or yellow pepper, seeded and diced
3 tbsp chopped fresh parsley
50 g (2 oz) raisins
40 g (1½ oz) cashew nuts, chopped
25 g (1 oz) Parmesan cheese, freshly grated

1 Preheat the oven to 180°C/350°F/gas mark 4.

2 Cut small lids from the top of the tomatoes and reserve. Scoop out and discard the seeds. Place the tomatoes upside-down on kitchen paper to drain.

3 Boil the rice in lightly salted water until just tender. Rinse in cold water and drain well.

4 Heat the oil and sauté the onion and garlic until soft and golden. Add the pepper and cook for 2 minutes. Remove from the heat and stir in the rice and remaining ingredients.

5 Divide the filling between the tomatoes. Replace the lids, put the tomatoes on a lightly oiled baking sheet and cook in the oven for 35–40 minutes. Serve hot or at room temperature.

Mustard-glazed rack of lamb

If possible, ask your butcher to trim the fat off the bone ends for you.

SERVES 6

3 racks of fat-trimmed lamb

salt and freshly ground black pepper

3 tbsp dry cider or white wine

3 tbsp honey-flavoured mustard

rosemary sprigs

1 Preheat the oven to 180°C/350°F/gas mark 4.

2 Score the fat of the lamb in a criss-cross pattern. Season and place in a small roasting tray. Mix the cider or wine with the mustard and spread some of the mixture over the lamb.

3 Place a couple of sprigs of rosemary on each rack of lamb and roast in the oven for 55–65 minutes until tender, brushing the lamb occasionally with more of the glaze.

Clockwise from front: mustard-glazed rack of lamb with baby carrots, garlic mash, stir-fried spinach.

Easter lamb pie

It is a good idea to prepare the filling for the pie in advance so that it has time to simmer gently until the meat is really tender, and cool completely before you assemble the pie.

SERVES 6

900 g (2 lb) boneless lamb, trimmed of fat
300 ml (10 fl oz) water
65 g (2½ oz) butter
juice of 1 lemon
1 bay leaf
1 cinnamon stick
a pinch of ground allspice
salt and freshly ground black pepper
1 tbsp oil
10–12 pickling onions or small shallots
250 g (9 oz) flat cap mushrooms, sliced
250 g (9 oz) small carrots, cut into 2.5 cm (1 in) lengths
1 tbsp plain flour
375 g (13 oz) puff pastry
1 egg beaten with 1 tbsp milk

1 Cut the lamb into 2.5 cm (1 in) cubes. Place the meat in a heavy-based pan with the water, 50 g (2 oz) of the butter, the lemon juice, bay leaf, cinnamon, allspice and seasoning. Bring to the boil, then part-cover and simmer very gently for 30–40 minutes or until the meat is very tender.

2 Meanwhile, heat the remaining butter and the oil in a pan and sauté the onions or shallots until golden. Add the mushrooms and carrots. Add a few spoonfuls of the stock from the meat and simmer gently for 30–40 minutes until the vegetables are tender.

3 Combine the meat and vegetables, adding a little water if necessary to make

Clockwise from top: Easter lamb pie, creamed leek potatoes, golden-top broccoli.

the stock up to 300 ml (10 fl oz). Blend the flour with a little water. Stir into the meat mixture and simmer for a few minutes to thicken, stirring continuously. Set aside until cold.

4 Preheat the oven to 220°C/425°F/gas mark 7.

5 Roll out the pastry to about 5 mm (¼ in) thick. Cut out a piece to cover the dish, then cut out an additional strip 2.5 cm (1 in) wide to line the rim of the dish. Moisten the rim with water and press the pastry strip on to it, overlapping the ends a little.

6 Spoon the filling into the dish and put a pie funnel in the centre. Brush the pastry rim with water. Lift the pastry lid, supporting it with the rolling pin, and place it over the pie. Seal the edges together with a fork. Brush with the egg and milk.

7 Bake in the oven for 25 minutes. Lower the oven temperature to 180°C/350°F/gas mark 4, cover the pie with foil and bake for a further 30 minutes. Serve hot.

Garlic mash and stir-fried spinach

You can prepare your vegetables while the lamb is roasting in the oven.

SERVES 6

FOR THE POTATOES

1.5 kg (3 lb) floury potatoes
2 garlic cloves, crushed
100 g (4 oz) butter, melted
4 tbsp single cream

FOR THE SPINACH

3 tbsp olive oil
2 red onions, thinly sliced
1 red pepper, cut into
    strips
450 g (1 lb) baby spinach
3 tbsp pine nuts, lightly
    toasted

1 Boil the potatoes in their skins until tender. Drain, peel and mash with the garlic, butter and cream.

2 Heat the oil in a large pan and fry the onion and pepper until just soft. Add the spinach and stir-fry quickly just until the spinach has wilted. Turn on to a warmed serving plate and garnish with the pine nuts.

Golden-top broccoli

You can also make this dish with cauliflower.

SERVES 6

2 eggs, hard-boiled
40 g (1½ oz) butter
6 tbsp fresh white bread-
    crumbs
1 tbsp finely chopped fresh
    parsley
salt and freshly ground
    black pepper
700–900 g (1½–2 lb)
    broccoli, divided into
    florets

Creamed leek potatoes

Adding leeks to creamy mashed potatoes gives them an extra flavour dimension. Choose a floury potato, such as Maris Piper, for best results.

SERVES 6

900 g (2 lb) potatoes,
    peeled and cut into
    chunks
450 g (1 lb) leeks
40 g (1½ oz) butter
3 tbsp double cream or
    crème fraîche
salt and freshly ground
    black pepper
3 tbsp snipped fresh chives

1 Put the potatoes in a pan of lightly salted water and bring to the boil.

2 Cut the leeks into quarters lengthways, then slice across thinly. When the potatoes are more than half cooked, add the leeks. Cook until very tender, then drain thoroughly.

3 Mash the vegetables with the butter. Beat in the cream or crème fraîche and seasoning. Serve sprinkled with chives.

1 Separate the eggs into whites and yolks. Finely chop the whites and mash the yolks.

2 Melt half the butter and fry the breadcrumbs until golden and crisp. Remove from the heat and stir in the parsley and seasoning.

3 Steam or boil the broccoli until tender but crisp. Drain, then toss in the remaining butter. Arrange in a dish and sprinkle with the breadcrumbs, egg whites and yolks.

Fresh fruit pavlova

For best results, make the meringue nest a day or two in advance and store it wrapped in foil in an airtight container.

SERVES 6

3 egg whites
175 g (6 oz) caster sugar
1 tbsp cider vinegar

FOR THE FILLING

300 ml (10 fl oz) double
    cream
150 ml (5 fl oz) crème
    fraîche
sugar to taste
1 large mango, chopped
3 kiwi fruit, sliced
100 g (4 oz) seedless
    grapes, halved

1 Preheat the oven to 160°C/325°F/gas mark 3. Draw a 20 cm (8 in) circle on a piece of baking parchment and lay it on a lightly greased baking sheet.

2 Beat the egg whites until they form stiff peaks. Add half the sugar, a tablespoon at a time, beating as you go. Fold in the remaining sugar and the vinegar using a metal spoon.

3 Spread a layer of meringue over the circle, then spoon or pipe the remaining meringue around the edge to make sides.

4 Bake in the oven for 45 minutes, covering with baking parchment if it starts to over-brown. Turn off the oven and leave the meringue in the oven until cold.

5 Shortly before serving, whip the cream until just forming peaks. Stir in the crème fraîche, sugar to taste and half the prepared fruit.

6 Fill the meringue nest with the fruit and cream mixture. Decorate with the remaining fruit and serve.

Amaretti and raspberry bombe

A distinctly Italian-style dessert, this makes a spectacular end to any celebratory meal.

SERVES 6–8

100 g (4 oz) Amaretti biscuits, crushed

6 tbsp Amaretti liqueur

250 g (9 oz) raspberries, lightly crushed

500 g (18 oz) Ricotta cheese

300 ml (10 fl oz) double cream

a pinch of salt

grated zest of 1 lemon

juice of $\frac{1}{2}$ lemon

caster sugar

a few mint sprigs

FOR THE FRUIT COULIS

250 g (9 oz) raspberries

120 ml (4 fl oz) orange juice

25–40 g (1–1$\frac{1}{2}$ oz) caster sugar

1 Line a 1.5 litre (2$\frac{1}{2}$ pint) mould or pudding basin with clingfilm and set aside.

2 Reserve a spoonful of the crushed biscuits to decorate, then mix the remainder with the liqueur and raspberries. Set aside.

3 Whisk the Ricotta with the cream and salt until thickened. Stir in the Amaretti mixture, lemon zest and juice, and add sugar to taste. Spoon the mixture into the prepared container and freeze for 3$\frac{1}{2}$–4 hours.

4 Reserve a few raspberries for decoration and process the remainder with the other coulis ingredients until smooth, then rub through a sieve to remove any seeds.

5 Shortly before serving, briefly dip the mould or basin in very hot water, then turn the bombe on to a dish. Scatter the reserved biscuits over the top of the bombe, then decorate with raspberries and mint sprigs and serve with the fruit coulis.

Iced carrot cake

Prepare this cake in advance as you need to begin decorating it the day before serving. If you don't trust your modelling skills, use chocolate eggs and decorate with fluffy chickens.

SERVES 6

275 g (10 oz) plain flour

2 tsp baking powder

1 tsp bicarbonate of soda

$\frac{1}{2}$ tsp ground cloves

$\frac{1}{2}$ tsp ground cinnamon

175 g (6 oz) carrots, grated

1 eating apple, peeled and grated

grated zest of 1 lemon

50 g (2 oz) sultanas

75 g (3 oz) pecan nuts, roughly chopped

175 g (6 oz) soft brown sugar

150 g (5 oz) sunflower margarine

3 eggs

FOR THE DECORATION

500 g (18 oz) ready-to-roll icing

food colouring

200 g (7 oz) almond paste

icing sugar, sifted

1 packet chocolate matchsticks

1 Preheat the oven to 180°C/350°F/gas mark 4. Grease and flour a 20 cm (8 in) square cake tin.

2 Sift together the flour, baking powder, bicarbonate of soda and ground spices.

3 In a separate bowl, mix the carrots, apples, lemon zest, sultanas and pecan nuts.

4 Beat together the sugar, margarine and eggs until light and fluffy. Fold in a little of the flour, then stir in the carrot mixture and the remaining flour mixture. Blend thoroughly.

5 Spoon the batter into the tin and bake in the oven for 1 hour or until a skewer inserted in the centre comes out clean. Turn out on to a rack to cool.

6 Roll out the icing between two sheets of clingfilm to 25 cm (10 in) square. Moisten the top and half the sides of the cake with water. Remove the top sheet of clingfilm and trim the icing. Use the clingfilm to lift up the icing and turn it on to the cake. Smooth down and remove the clingfilm. Shape the corners to look like a tablecloth.

7 Using food colouring and a brush, paint a pattern on to the icing. Leave overnight to dry.

8 Colour small pieces of the almond paste, and make tiny Easter eggs and chicks. Add a little icing sugar if it gets sticky. Set aside on a surface dusted with icing sugar or on a sheet of clingfilm.

9 Make a nest in the centre of the cake by placing six chocolate matchstick halves in a hexagon shape. Place a second layer of matchsticks on top, each one resting across a corner of the hexagon. Repeat until the nest is four layers high. Then fill with eggs and chicks.

Christmas Favourites

It's the highlight of the year and you'll enjoy it whatever you eat, but to keep it really special, make sure everything goes to plan with these failsafe dishes for the holiday season.

We've provided a whole range of exciting recipes for Christmas so that you can mix and match those to suit your celebration.

There are traditional and more unusual ideas for main courses and vegetables, plus some delectable puddings for your Christmas Day meal.

Traditional Turkey Dinner

URKEY WITH *all the trimmings is the essence of Christmas dinner. Try a new selection of vegetables to keep the flavours fresh and exciting.*

Menu for eight

BLOODY MARY SOUP WITH MELBA TOAST
—
ROAST TURKEY WITH STUFFING
AND PERFECT GRAVY

PAPRIKA ROAST POTATOES

CREAMY CARROT MASH

SPROUTS WITH CHESTNUTS

BREAD SAUCE

Bloody Mary soup with melba toast

If you don't want to make the melba toast, just serve the soup with crusty bread.

SERVES 8

3 tbsp olive oil
1 large onion, chopped
3 bacon rashers, chopped
3 celery sticks, chopped
2 garlic cloves, chopped
1.2 litres (2 pints) tomato juice
1 tbsp caster sugar
2 bay leaves
1 tbsp lemon juice
salt and freshly ground black pepper

TO SERVE

8–12 slices medium white bread
8 celery sticks
Tabasco sauce
Worcestershire sauce
2 lemons, cut into wedges
celery salt
250 ml (8 fl oz) vodka (optional)

1 Heat the oil and gently fry the onion, bacon, celery and garlic for 10 minutes.

2 Add the tomato juice, sugar and bay leaves, bring to the boil, then cover and simmer for 20 minutes. Remove the bay leaves.

3 Blend in a liquidizer, then rub through a sieve. Season with lemon juice, salt and pepper and reheat gently.

4 Meanwhile, toast the bread on each side. While it is still warm, cut off the crusts and split the bread horizontally into two thinner pieces. Place the uncooked side under the grill for a few seconds to brown.

5 Serve the soup and melba toast with celery, Tabasco and Worcestershire sauces, lemon wedges and celery salt so that guests can spice up their own portions. Add vodka shots for extra Christmas spirit.

How to roast the perfect turkey

Cooking a turkey is not difficult, but you must allow plenty of time for the bird to cook thoroughly and plan for it to be cooked 45 minutes before serving.

1 Preheat the oven to 190°C/375°F/gas mark 5.

2 Brush the bird with butter and cover with foil. Calculate the cooking time based on 20–25 minutes per 450 g (1 lb) plus 20 minutes or 40 minutes per 1 kg (2¼ lb) plus 40 minutes. A 4.5 kg (10 lb) turkey therefore needs 3–4 hours' cooking.

3 After the first 2½ hours, remove the foil, season well and baste with the cooking juices. Return to the oven until cooked through.

4 Once cooked, cover lightly with foil to allow the steam to escape and leave to rest until you are ready to carve.

Perfect gravy

Make plenty of gravy to serve with your roast meat. Take all but 3–4 tbsp of fat from the roasting tin. Stir in enough flour to form a thick roux, then gradually pour in 1 litre (1¾ pints) of chicken stock and stir continuously over a medium heat. Once the gravy has thickened, strain it into a pan and cook over a low heat for another 10 minutes, stirring regularly. It's a good idea to make the gravy well in advance so there's enough time for the flour to be fully integrated into the mixture.

Quick and easy stuffings

If you don't have time to make your own, buy a good-quality packet stuffing and add one or two extras to jazz it up. Try some of these ideas:

- finely grated zest of 1 orange;

- a handful of sultanas;

- a few slices of chopped Parma ham;

- 3–4 tbsp roughly chopped fresh parsley.

- 75 g (3 oz) cooked wild rice.

Paprika roast potatoes

These are crisp on the outside with a hint of paprika to spice up the taste and add colour to the meal.

SERVES 8

200 ml (7 fl oz) walnut oil
32 King Edward or Maris Piper potatoes, peeled
plain flour
paprika
salt and freshly ground black pepper

1 Preheat the oven to 200°C/400°F/gas mark 6. Place the oil in a roasting tin and place in the oven.

2 Parboil the potatoes for 10 minutes, then drain. Pierce the surface of each potato with a fork, then lightly sprinkle with flour, paprika and seasoning. Gently place in the hot oil and cook for 45 minutes until tender and crisp, turning once.

SETTING THE SCENE
Blue china with a crisp snowflake pattern is perfect for the Christmas table and we combined it with white and silver and added touches of opulent purple and festive orange.

Creamy carrot mash

This is the ideal accompaniment when you are entertaining, as everything can be done in advance.

SERVES 8

900 g (2 lb) carrots, cooked
450 g (1 lb) swede, cooked
1 tbsp olive oil
100 g (4 oz) cream cheese
salt and freshly ground black pepper
1 tsp caraway seeds

1 Purée the carrots and swede with the oil, half the cream cheese, the salt and pepper.

2 About 30 minutes before serving, place the mixture in an ovenproof dish with the remaining cheese in the centre and the caraway seeds sprinkled on top. Place in the bottom of the oven to reheat and give the mash the right consistency.

Clockwise from top: roast turkey, sprouts with chestnuts, creamy carrot mash and bread sauce

Sprouts with chestnuts

The secret to cooking the perfect Brussels sprouts is not to boil them for too long. They should be just tender but still crisp and nutty.

SERVES 8

900 g (2 lb) Brussels
   sprouts
50 g (2 oz) butter
250 g (9 oz) ready-prepared
   chestnuts
salt and freshly ground
   black pepper

1 Cook the sprouts in boiling water for about 10 minutes until just firm but still crisp. Drain and set aside.

2 Melt the butter in a large frying pan until sizzling. Add the sprouts and chestnuts and stir-fry quickly to heat through and coat in the butter. Season to taste and serve at once.

Sprouts and chestnuts stir-fried in butter.

Bread sauce

Home-made bread sauce is very easy to make and the perfect accompaniment to your Christmas meal. If you want, you can make it in advance then simply reheat and finish it off just before you serve.

SERVES 8

1 onion
8 cloves
900 g (1½ pints) full-fat milk
10 white peppercorns
2 bay leaves
½ tsp grated nutmeg
175 g (6 oz) fresh white
   breadcrumbs
75 g (3 oz) butter, melted
4 tbsp single cream
salt and freshly ground
   black pepper

1 Halve the onion and press the cloves into it. Put in a pan with the milk, peppercorns, bay leaves and nutmeg. Slowly bring to the boil, then simmer for 15 minutes.

2 Strain the milk, discarding the onion, then stir in the breadcrumbs.

3 If you are serving the sauce straight away, drizzle the butter and cream over the top and season. If you are making it in advance, add them when you reheat the sauce.

Creamy carrot mash and a traditional bread sauce.

Dress up ready-made cranberry sauce with a few fresh cranberries.

A Bird for Each Guest

Menu for six

FOR A TOUCH of sophistication, serve poussins as an alternative to turkey, so that everyone has a miniature bird to themselves – and you don't have to carve!

TARRAGON POUSSINS WITH
STUFFED PUMPKINS

GOLDEN POTATO CAKE

GLAZED TURNIPS AND CARROTS

STEAMED BEANS WITH ASPARAGUS SPEARS

Tarragon poussins with stuffed pumpkins

The very Christmassy flavours of orange and cloves perfectly complement the delicate flavour of the poussins and everyone can have their own individual roast bird.

SERVES 6

6 poussins

salt and freshly ground black pepper

1 large orange, broken into six wedges

24 whole cloves

a large bunch of tarragon

100 g (4 oz) butter, softened

1 tbsp paprika

juice of 1 large orange

175–200 g (6–7 oz) baby pumpkins

100 g (4 oz) back bacon

5 tbsp oil

100 g (4 oz) eating apples, cored and diced

1½ tsp ground coriander

200 g (7 oz) watercress, finely chopped

175 g (6 oz) fresh breadcrumbs

200 ml (7 fl oz) single cream

2 oranges, sliced

a few flatleaf parsley sprigs

1 Preheat the oven to 190°C/375°F/gas mark 5.

2 Wipe the poussins with kitchen paper and season inside. Stud the orange wedges with cloves and place one in each bird with a sprig of tarragon. Rub the butter into the skins and sprinkle with paprika. Place in a roasting tray and drizzle with orange juice.

3 Roast the poussins at the top of the oven for 35 minutes.

4 Meanwhile, cut off and reserve the lids from the pumpkins. Remove the seeds and membranes. Parboil the pumpkins for 3–4 minutes, then drain.

5 Sauté the bacon gently in 3 tbsp of the oil. Add the apple and coriander and sauté briefly. Stir in the watercress and breadcrumbs and season with pepper.

6 Divide the stuffing between the pumpkins and replace the lids. Rub with the remaining oil and place in a roasting tray. Place in the oven below the poussins and continue to roast for a further 10 minutes until cooked through and golden.

7 Arrange the pumpkins and poussins on a warmed serving platter and keep warm.

Clockwise from top: potato cake, glazed turnips and carrots, steamed beans with asparagus spears, tarragon poussins with stuffed pumpkins.

8 Pour any excess fat from the poussins tray and remove the sediment. Stir in the cream and bring to simmering point over a medium heat, stirring. Strain into a pan and keep warm. Stir in 1 tbsp of chopped fresh tarragon and pour into a warmed bowl.

9 Garnish the poussins with orange slices, tarragon and flatleaf parsley and serve with the sauce.

Golden potato cake

This can be made a day in advance and allowed to cool, then kept on a baking tray in foil in the fridge. Reheat at 190°C/375°F/gas mark 5 for 20–25 minutes until the cake is heated through.

SERVES 6

50 g (2 oz) butter

1 onion, finely chopped

1.5 kg (3 lb) Desirée or similar potatoes, peeled

100 g (4 oz) mild Cheddar or Gruyère cheese, grated

salt and freshly ground black pepper

2 tbsp chopped fresh parsley

1 Preheat the oven to 180°C/350°F/gas mark 4. Grease a 20 cm (8 in) fixed-base sandwich tin and line with baking parchment, using a double layer for the base.

2 Melt the butter and sauté the onion over low heat until soft and translucent.

3 Wash the potatoes and slice thinly, but do not wash again. Place a quarter in the base of the tin. Spoon over one-third of the onions with the butter. Sprinkle with one-third of the cheese and season. Repeat twice, using all the onion and cheese, then finish with a layer of potatoes.

Above: *A mixture of steamed French and broad beans and asparagus, tossed in butter.*

Below left: *Golden potato cake makes a change from the traditional roast variety.*

4 Press down the potatoes and cover with a double layer of oiled parchment. Bake in the oven for 1½ hours, removing the top paper for the last 20 minutes. When cooked, run a spatula along the side of the tin and remove the paper from the sides.

5 Press down the potatoes firmly with a spatula, then grill for 4–5 minutes.

6 Loosen the edge again and turn on to a flame-proof dish. Place under the grill until the other side is golden brown. Serve garnished with parsley.

Glazed turnips and carrots

If you cannot find baby turnips, just cut larger vegetables into chunks.

SERVES 6

450 g (1 lb) baby turnips

450 g (1 lb) baby carrots

75 g (3 oz) butter

salt and freshly ground black pepper

1 Boil the turnips in lightly salted water for about 10 minutes until tender. Meanwhile boil the carrots in lightly salted water for about 5 minutes until just tender. Drain well.

2 Melt the butter in a large pan, add the vegetables and toss together well until coated in butter and beginning to brown slightly.

Steamed beans with asparagus spears

As a short cut, you can use ready-prepared frozen broad beans to make this dish really quick and easy.

SERVES 6

350 g (12 oz) French beans

350 g (12 oz) shelled broad beans

450 g (1 lb) asparagus spears

75 g (3 oz) butter, melted

salt and freshly ground black pepper

1 Cook the vegetables separately in lightly salted boiling water until just tender. Drain well.

2 Transfer all the vegetables to a warmed serving dish and toss with the butter and a little pepper.

Perfect Puddings

*S*PICY FRUIT, *melting chocolate and the best mince pies you've ever tasted – all the ingredients for a final flourish.*

Decorate your Christmas pudding with delicious caramelized physalis (see caramelized fruit page 96).

Christmas pudding with three sauces

Buy a good-quality ready-made Christmas pudding and serve with any or all three accompaniments

Brandy butter

Use a good-quality unsalted butter for best results and add brandy to suit your own taste.

SERVES 6

150 g (5 oz) unsalted butter
50 g (2 oz) caster sugar
50 g (2 oz) icing sugar
6–10 tbsp brandy
ground cinnamon

1 Beat the butter until creamy, then gradually beat in the sugars until light and fluffy.

2 Add the brandy a tablespoon at a time, sprinkle with cinnamon and serve at room temperature.

Rum sauce

You really need to taste this sauce as you add the rum so that you can add as much or as little as you and your guests prefer. If you really like to go heavy on the spirit, remember to make something else for the children!

SERVES 6

25 g (1 oz) cornflour
600 ml (1 pint) milk
25 g (1 oz) butter
2 tbsp soft brown sugar
4–8 tbsp rum

1 Mix the cornflour to a smooth paste with a little of the cold milk.

2 Bring the remaining milk to the boil in a pan. Pour over the cornflour paste, mix thoroughly, then return to the pan. Cook over a low heat, stirring constantly until the sauce thickens.

3 Remove the pan from the heat and stir in the butter, sugar and rum to taste. Serve the sauce warm.

Mascarpone cream

Rich and creamy Italian Mascarpone cheese is readily available in supermarkets and perfect for indulgent dessert sauces.

SERVES 6

450 g (1 lb) Mascarpone cheese
150 ml (5 fl oz) double cream
4 tbsp caster sugar
1 tbsp vanilla essence

1 Beat the cheese until soft, then gradually beat in the cream, sugar and vanilla essence. Spoon into a freezer container and freeze overnight.

2 Remove from the freezer 30 minutes before required.

Moreish mince pies

It's really worth making the pastry for this recipe if you have time. The addition of cream and lemon makes the pastry light and flaky and produces irresistible mince pies.

MAKES 24

175 g (6 oz) butter, diced
300 g (10 oz) plain flour
1 tsp salt
4 tbsp double cream
grated zest of 2 lemons
2 tbsp cold water
450 g (1 lb) good-quality
    mincemeat

1 Rub the butter into the flour and salt in a large mixing bowl.

2 Add the cream, lemon zest and water and mix to a smooth dough. Be careful not to overwork the pastry. Cover and leave to rest for 30 minutes.

3 Preheat the oven to 200°C/400°/gas mark 6. Grease a mince-pie tray.

4 Roll out the pastry to 5 mm ($\frac{1}{4}$ in) thick. Use larger rounds to line the tins, spoon 2 tsp of mincemeat into each one, lightly moisten the pastry edges with water and top with smaller rounds. Prick the tops with a fork.

5 Bake in the centre of the oven for 20–25 minutes until the pastry is pale and golden brown.

Caramelized fruit

Dip physalis, figs, dates or other fruit into sugar caramel and use them as toppings or sweetmeats.

SERVES 6

6 small satsumas, clemen-
    tines or other Christmas
    citrus fruit, peeled but
    left whole
250 g (9 oz) caster sugar

1 Wash the fruit well. Place in a heavy-based pan with the sugar and enough water to cover the top. Bring to the boil and simmer without a lid for about 20 minutes or until the fruit collapses.

2 Remove the fruit and boil the remaining liquid to form a golden caramel, without allowing it to go too brown. Pour the liquid over the fruit and serve with ice cream, leftover brandy butter or rum sauce.

Chocolate and chestnut log

A yule log with a difference, this light chocolate creation has a rich chestnut filling laced with Grand Marnier.

SERVES 6

5 large eggs, separated
100 g (4 oz) caster sugar
75 g (3 oz) plain flour
50 g (2 oz) cocoa powder

FOR THE FILLING

75 g (3 oz) prepared sweet chestnuts, chopped, or 75 g (3 oz) tinned chestnut purée
2 tbsp Grand Marnier or brandy
1 tbsp fresh orange juice
200 ml (7 fl oz) crème fraîche
75 g (3 oz) white chocolate drops or diced white chocolate

FOR THE ICING

150 g (5 oz) plain chocolate drops or diced chocolate
65 g (2½ oz) unsalted butter
3 tbsp double cream

TO DECORATE

chocolate holly leaves
silver dragees
icing sugar, sifted

1 Preheat the oven to 220°C/425°F/gas mark 7. Line a 23 × 33 cm (9 × 13 in) Swiss roll tin with baking parchment and grease the parchment.

2 Whisk egg yolks with the sugar until pale and fluffy.

3 Sift together the flour and half the cocoa. Whisk the egg whites until they form soft peaks. Mix the flour into the egg yolks. Fold in a quarter of the egg whites, then gently fold in the remainder. Pour the batter into the tin and bake in the oven for 10 minutes.

4 Turn out on to a sheet of parchment dusted with the remaining cocoa. Peel off the lining paper. Working from one short end, roll up the sponge with the cocoa parchment. Wrap loosely in another sheet of parchment and allow to cool.

5 Purée the chestnuts, liqueur, orange juice and 1–2 tbsp of crème fraîche.

6 Melt the white chocolate in a heatproof bowl over a pan of barely simmering water. Leave to cool a little. Mix in the flavoured chestnut purée.

7 Unroll the cake and remove the baking parchment. Spread with the chestnut filling and carefully re-roll. Wrap loosely in foil and chill.

8 Melt the plain chocolate and butter in a heatproof bowl over a pan of barely simmering water, stirring frquently. Leave to cool a little, then stir in the cream and leave to cool completely.

9 Spread the icing over the log and leave to set. Decorate with chocolate holly leaves, silver dragees and icing sugar.

Boxing Day Delights

A CENTREPIECE HAM *is always popular, and can be served cold throughout the holiday. Tangy fruit desserts and non-alcoholic drinks provide a refreshing alternative to all the over-indulgence of the season.*

Damson-glazed ham

Order the ham from your butcher to ensure you get the cut and weight you want. There should be plenty left for cold cuts, pies or quiches for the rest of the holiday.

SERVES 6

1 x 4.5 kg–7.5 kg (10–17 lb) cooked ham
200 g (7 oz) damson or plum jam
2 tbsp soft brown sugar
1 tbsp water
25 g (1 oz) glacé cherries, halved
whole cloves

1 Preheat the oven to 230°C/450°F/gas mark 8.

2 Remove the rind from the ham and score a diamond pattern in the thin layer of fat underneath. Place the ham in a roasting tin.

3 Warm the jam with the sugar and water, then rub through a sieve. Brush the warm jam over the joint.

4 Roast the ham in the oven for 30–35 minutes until the fat is crisp and golden brown.

5 Secure the glacé cherry halves in each diamond with a whole clove.

Sweet and sour spiced shallots

These can be prepared up to a week in advance and stored in the fridge. They are also delicious with cold cuts.

SERVES 6

120 ml (4 fl oz) olive oil
500 g (18 oz) shallots
50 g (2 oz) raisins
1 tbsp yellow mustard seeds
½ tsp black peppercorns, crushed
a few blades of mace
50 g (2 oz) caster sugar
120 ml (4 fl oz) red wine vinegar
a pinch of salt

1 Heat the oil in a shallow, lidded pan. Cook the shallots, raisins, mustard seeds, peppercorns and mace over a low heat for 30 minutes, removing any smaller shallots that cook quickly.

2 Remove all the shallots from the pan and add the sugar, vinegar and a pinch of salt. Boil fast for 3–4 minutes, then pour the syrup over the shallots. Cool, cover and chill.

Sweet potato purée

Sweet potatoes, with their attractive orange flesh, are increasingly available in supermarkets.

SERVES 6

1.5 kg (3 lb) sweet potatoes, peeled and cut into chunks
50–75 g (2–3 oz) butter
salt and freshly ground black pepper
snipped fresh chives or parsley

1 Boil the potatoes in lightly salted water for about 15 minutes until tender. Drain thouroughly.

2 Mash with butter and seasoning. Garnish with chives or parsley.

Opposite: *Damson-glazed ham with sweet and sour spiced shallots and sweet potato purée.*

Pannacotta with fresh fruit salad

Make the pannacotta a day in advance. For a softer consistency, use 2 tsp of gelatine. Fresh fruit salad makes a wonderful accompaniment.

SERVES 6

200 ml (7 fl oz) full-fat milk
zest of 1 lemon
$\frac{1}{2}$ tsp vanilla essence
50 g (2 oz) caster sugar
1 tbsp powdered gelatine
300 ml (10 fl oz) double
   cream
selection of fresh fruits such
   as figs, satsumas and
   cranberries
caster sugar (optional)

1 Place the milk, lemon zest, vanilla essence and sugar in a pan and bring to a simmer. Stir to dissolve the sugar, then remove from the heat and leave to stand for 30 minutes.

2 Sprinkle the gelatine into the cream, stir and add to the milk. Bring to a simmer, ensuring that the gelatine has dissolved. Strain and use to fill six tiny non-stick or plastic moulds. Leave to cool, then cover and chill.

3 Dip the moulds in hot water and shake to loosen the pannacotta. Turn out on to a dish.

4 Prepare and combine the fruits to make a salad and sprinkle with a little caster sugar, if liked.

Harlequin pears

Serve these delicious fruits cold with whipped cream or ice cream.

SERVES 6

250 ml (8 fl oz) fresh
   orange juice
75 g (3 oz) caster sugar
1 cinnamon stick
zest from $\frac{1}{2}$ lemon
8 tbsp cranberry sauce
6 x 225–250 g (8–9 oz)
   ripe, firm William pears
75 g (3 oz) pecan nuts,
   chopped

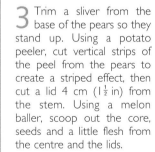

1 Preheat the oven to 200°C/400°F/gas mark 6.

2 Bring the orange juice, sugar, cinnamon, lemon zest and 2 tbsp of cranberry sauce to the boil and cook until syrupy. Strain and set aside.

3 Trim a sliver from the base of the pears so they stand up. Using a potato peeler, cut vertical strips of the peel from the pears to create a striped effect, then cut a lid 4 cm (1$\frac{1}{2}$ in) from the stem. Using a melon baller, scoop out the core, seeds and a little flesh from the centre and the lids.

4 Mix the nuts and remaining cranberry sauce and pour into the pears. Replace the lids and place the pears in a shallow dish. Drizzle with the syrup and bake in the oven for 30–35 minutes until tender when tested with a skewer, basting occasionally with the syrup. Leave to cool.

Clockwise from top: moreish mince pies (see page 96), fresh fruit salad, pannacotta.

Food of the gods

Buy fresh figs when they are just soft, wash well, then simply take off the stem. Try different-flavoured flower honeys to vary the recipe.

SERVES 6–8

8 fresh figs, chopped
750 ml (1¼ pints) Greek yoghurt
5 tbsp clear honey

1 Divide the figs between individual bowls or dessert plates and add a scoop of yoghurt.

2 Warm a metal spoon, then use it to drizzle a little honey over the top of each bowl.

Cranberry cooler

This traditional American drink is a great non-alcoholic alternative for Christmas.

SERVES 6–8

1 litre (1¾ pints) cranberry juice
juice of 4 large pink grapefruits
crushed ice

1 Rinse eight tumblers in cold water and place them in the freezer for 5 minutes.

2 In a large jug, combine the cranberry and grapefruit juice with the crushed ice.

3 Remove the glasses from the freezer, pour in the juice and serve immediately.

Holiday Treats

*I*F YOU *are spending a day during the holidays just with the family or close friends, you'll want a more informal menu — so here's a selection of dishes which are simplicity itself to prepare, including great ideas for using up the remains of the Christmas Day turkey.*

Stuffed tomatoes

Small beefsteak tomatoes are just the right size for this dish and are easier to manage than smaller tomatoes.

SERVES 6

225 g (8 oz) smoked
   haddock fillet
6 small beefsteak tomatoes
5 tbsp fromage frais
100 g (4 oz) cooked peeled
   prawns
1 tbsp wholegrain mustard
4 tbsp snipped fresh chives

1 Preheat the oven to 190°C/375°F/gas mark 5. Line a baking sheet with greaseproof paper.

2 Place the haddock in a shallow pan, cover with water and simmer for 1–2 minutes. Lift out, remove and discard the skin and bones, and flake the flesh.

3 Cut out and discard a small lid from the stalk end of the tomatoes. Scoop out the seeds and core. Drain the tomatoes upside-down on kitchen paper.

4 Place the tomatoes on the baking sheet and bake in the oven for 15–20 minutes until just soft; do not overcook. Drain upside-down on kitchen paper. Keep the tomatoes warm.

5 Warm the fromage frais, prawns and mustard very gently over low heat. Add the flaked haddock, heat through gently and stir in 3 tbsp of chives. Place the tomatoes on a serving dish and pile with the filling. Garnish with the remaining chives.

Spicy pilaf

This has a mildly Middle Eastern flavour – you will get perfect, fluffy rice if you follow the simple instructions.

SERVES 6

350 g (12 oz) basmati rice
50 g (2 oz) butter
2 shallots, finely chopped
a pinch of saffron strands
1 bay leaf
175–225 g (6–8 oz) cooked turkey or chicken, skinned and diced (optional)
75 g (3 oz) raisins
75 g (3 oz) natural cashew nuts, roughly chopped
500 ml (18 fl oz) chicken or vegetable stock
salt and freshly ground black pepper
2 tbsp chopped fresh flatleaf parsley

1 Place the rice in a strainer and wash well. Place in a bowl, cover with cold water and set aside for 15–20 minutes, then drain well.

2 Meanwhile, melt the butter and sauté the shallots over a low heat until soft. Add the saffron, bay leaf, turkey or chicken, raisins, nuts and drained rice.

3 Pour in the stock, season and bring to the boil. Cover tightly and simmer for 15–18 minutes without lifting the lid.

4 Remove from the heat and leave to stand undisturbed for 3–5 minutes. Fork through the rice, adding a little extra butter if desired, and serve garnished with parsley.

Ham and cheese baguettes

Endlessly adaptable, this basic recipe is a great one for quick holiday lunches and suppers.

SERVES 6

3 mini baguettes, halved lengthways
50 g (2 oz) butter
6 large, thick slices of ham
1 tbsp Dijon mustard
1 large eating apple, thinly sliced
225 g (8 oz) Gruyère cheese, coarsely grated

1 Preheat the oven to 230°C/450°F/gas mark 8.

2 Lightly butter the baguettes. Top with thick slices of ham and spread with a little mustard to taste. Arrange a few apple slices on top and sprinkle with a generous layer of cheese.

3 Bake in the oven for 12–15 minutes until crisp and golden brown. Serve hot.

Rainbow pasta

This dish doesn't have to be served piping hot, so it works well as part of a buffet.

SERVES 6

450 g (1 lb) multi-coloured spaghetti or other pasta shapes

450 g (1 lb) frozen sliced mixed peppers, thawed

salt and freshly ground black pepper

450 g (1 lb) cooked turkey, shredded

900 ml (1½ pints) ready-made or home-made white sauce

100 g (4 oz) Cheddar or Cheshire cheese

50 g (2 oz) whole almonds or cashew nuts

1 tbsp chopped fresh herbs

1 Preheat the oven to 200°C/400°F/gas mark 6.

2 Cook the pasta in boiling, salted water, then drain well and mix with the peppers. Season and spread over the bottom of a well-greased ovenproof dish.

3 Add the turkey pieces and pour over the sauce. Sprinkle with cheese and nuts and bake for 20–30 minutes until the cheese is crisp and golden. Garnish with fresh herbs and serve.

Winter salad

After all the over-indulgence, your guests will welcome a crisp salad and this colourful recipe has enough bite to satisfy jaded palates. Pink peppercorns are available from good supermarkets and delicatessens.

SERVES 6

1 small or ½ large white cabbage, shredded

1 red onion, shredded

175 g (6 oz) Stilton cheese, diced

50–75 ml (2–3 fl oz) olive oil

1 tbsp pickled pink peppercorns

1 large bunch of fresh flatleaf parsley, roughly chopped

½ tsp fennel seeds

salt and freshly ground black pepper

Lightly toss all the ingredients together. Season well and serve immediately.

Crumble-top cake

The crumble topping for this sponge cake is a deliciously spiced mixture of demerara sugar, butter, ginger, cinnamon and almonds.

SERVES 6

FOR THE TOPPING

50 g (2 oz) plain flour

65 g (2½ oz) demerara sugar

1 tsp ground ginger

1 tsp ground cinnamon

25 g (1 oz) almonds, finely chopped

50 g (2 oz) butter

FOR THE SPONGE

190 g (6½ oz) butter

250 g (9 oz) plain flour

75 g (3 oz) potato flour or cornflour

3 tbsp baking powder

a pinch of salt

175 g (6 oz) caster sugar

2 large eggs

135 ml (4½ fl oz) milk

icing sugar, sifted

1 Preheat the oven to 190°C/375°F/gas mark 5.

2 Mix the flour, sugar, spices and almonds, then rub in the butter until the mixture is crumbly.

3 Grease a loose-bottomed 20 cm (8 in) cake tin with about 15 g (½ oz) of the butter. Dust with a little of the flour and set aside.

4 Sift together the flours, baking powder and salt. Beat the remaining butter with the sugar until light and fluffy. Beat in the eggs and the flour mixture, then gradually add the milk.

5 Spoon the batter into the cake tin. Scatter the crumble mixture over the top and bake in the oven for about 45 minutes.

6 Turn out the cake and leave to cool. Serve dusted with icing sugar while still warm or allow to cool, wrap in a double layer of foil and store in an airtight container.

Quick Party Canapés

F INGER FOOD *is the easiest way to enter-tain — and is also a family treat if you want a break from formal round-the-table meals.*

Roasted pepper and Mozzarella wraps

You can buy tapenade in all good supermarkets. It is a pâté made of black olives, garlic and anchovies.

MAKES ABOUT 20

3 long red peppers
extra virgin olive oil
50 g (2 oz) tapenade or black olive pâté
250 g (9 oz) Mozzarella cheese, cut into thin batons

1 Preheat the oven to 240°C/475°F/gas mark 9.

2 Place the peppers on a baking tray, drizzle with a little of the oil and roast in the oven for about 20 minutes until the skin is wrinkled and slightly charred. Place in a plastic bag and leave to cool.

3 Peel off and discard the skins and seeds. Slice the flesh of each pepper into 6–7 long, thin strips, cutting from stalk to tip. Dry on kitchen paper.

4 Spread the pepper strips with tapenade or olive pâté on the insides. Roll the strips around the cheese batons and secure with cocktail sticks. Drizzle a little oil over the top and serve.

Double-decker salmon blinis

The quantities of a canapé like this are not crucial – you can make as many or as few as you like.

MAKES ABOUT 35

about 20 blinis, cut into seventy 4 cm (1½ in) rounds
250 ml (8 fl oz) crème fraîche
225 g (8 oz) smoked salmon, cut into thin strips
50 g (2 oz) black lumpfish roe (optional)
chopped fresh dill or chives

1 Preheat the oven to 180°C/350°F/gas mark 4.

2 Place the blinis on a baking sheet and heat for 15 minutes.

3 Remove from the oven and place on a work surface. Spread crème fraîche on each one and top with salmon. Place one blini on top of another and garnish with lumpfish roe, dill or chives.

Aubergine goats' cheese rolls

The classic Italian combination of garlic, basil and pine nuts in the pesto is the perfect complement to the aubergines and mild goats' cheese. You may want to be more generous with your pesto.

MAKES ABOUT 30

2 long aubergines

1 tsp salt

50 g (2 oz) pesto sauce

250 g (8 oz) mild goats' cheese, cut into chunks

4–5 tbsp extra virgin olive oil

2 tbsp lemon juice

1 Cut the aubergines slightly on the diagonal into 15–16 oval, 5 mm ($\frac{1}{4}$ in) thick slices. Place in a bowl, toss with the salt, then set aside for 30–45 minutes. Rinse in cold water and pat dry.

2 Preheat the oven to 180°C/350°F/gas mark 4.

3 Spread one side of each aubergine slice generously with pesto. Roll each slice around a knob of cheese and secure with a cocktail sticks.

4 Mix the oil and lemon juice. Spoon a little into a large, shallow ovenproof dish, arrange the aubergine rolls in single layer, then drizzle with the remaining oil and lemon juice. Cover with foil and bake in the oven for 30–40 minutes, brushing with extra oil during cooking if necessary. Serve hot or at room temperature.

Quickest canapés

The next three recipe ideas are the quickest canapés of all. For best results, don't make them more than 1 $\frac{1}{2}$ hours before serving. Once made, cover them with foil or clingfilm and chill until you are ready to serve.

Antipasto on sticks

Cut thinly sliced prosciutto into three pieces. Halve slices of bresaola and thinly sliced salami. Gather the pieces into decorative shapes and thread on to thin wooden skewers, interspersing the meat with melon cubes, stuffed olives, seedless grapes or similar fruit, avoiding fruit that discolours.

Mini salmon roe tartlets

Spoon fromage frais into tiny, ready-made pastry cases. Top each case with $\frac{1}{2}$ tsp of salmon roe and garnish with some snipped fresh chives.

Clockwise from top left: antipasto on sticks, double-decker salmon blinis, spicy cucumber prawns, mini salmon roe tartlets, roasted pepper and Mozzarella wraps, aubergine goats' cheese rolls.

Spicy cucumber prawns

Cut a cucumber slightly on the diagonal into 5 mm ($\frac{1}{4}$ in) thick oval slices and pat dry on kitchen paper. Blend some mayonnaise with a little chilli sauce and a crushed garlic clove to taste. Spoon this on to the centre of each cucumber slice. Top each one with a cooked, peeled tiger prawn (preferably with the tail still on), freshly ground black pepper and snipped fresh chives.

PARTY TRICKS
Use gold-edged plates or scalloped gold doilies to present the canapés. For a quick mini-sweet, serve a plate of white and plain chocolate truffles dusted with icing sugar and decorated with holly.

Eating

Alfresco

THESE MENUS take summer that bit further. They are all designed for when the weather is good enough for you to take the table outside and enjoy the sheer pleasure of eating alfresco. Whether it's a casual picnic eaten with your fingers or an elegant dinner served in the garden, make the most of all the sunshine flavours available – and look for clever containers to make transport and serving that much easier.

The Potted Picnic

THE REASON sandwiches are such practical picnic food is that they provide their own 'packaging', ready to transport. This menu continues the theme with a few new twists, adding deliciously filled pittas and croissants — and the perfect picnic pudding-on-a-stick.

Marinated olives

These are best prepared the day before and can be stored in the fridge for up to two weeks.

SERVES 6

300 g (10 oz) stoned olives in brine
6–10 birds' eye chilli peppers
2 tbsp roughly chopped fresh rosemary
2 tsp fennel seeds
2–3 star anise seeds
2–3 cardamom seeds
enough olive oil to cover the olives

1 Drain the olives, rinse with cold water and drain well on kitchen paper.

2 In a large Kilner or screw-topped jar, place the olives, chilli peppers, rosemary, fennel, star anise and cardamom, and add enough olive oil to ensure that all the olives are covered.

3 Seal and store in the fridge for 2 weeks

Onion and potato frittata

This can be made a day in advance, transported whole to the picnic and cut into chunks once you get there. Protect it during travelling by lining the frying pan it was cooked in with greaseproof paper, laying the frittata on top and covering it with clingfilm.

SERVES 6

3 tbsp olive oil
3 onions, thinly sliced
6–10 new potatoes, cooked and halved
10 eggs
salt and freshly ground black pepper
a small handful of basil leaves, shredded

1 Heat 2 tbsp of the oil and gently fry the onions for about 15 minutes in a 25 cm (10 in) frying pan.

2 Add the potatoes and cook with the onions for a further 5 minutes.

3 Meanwhile, whisk the eggs and season well.

4 Add the remaining oil to the pan and once it's hot, pour on the egg mixture and scatter with the shredded basil leaves.

5 Cook gently, easing the egg away from the sides of the pan with a spatula as it sets, allowing uncooked egg to run to the side of the pan. Continue this process until the egg is almost all set.

6 The centre will still be quite runny and this can be set by placing the pan under a medium grill for a few minutes.

7 Allow the frittata to sit in the pan to cool slightly before serving.

Sage and onion sausage rolls

Classic favourites with a dash of extra flavour. If you're using fresh sausagemeat and pastry, then you can make the rolls in advance and freeze them uncooked (without the egg glaze). Increase the cooking time by 10 minutes if preparing them from frozen.

SERVES 6

250 g (9 oz) sausagemeat
1 large onion, finely chopped
2 tbsp chopped fresh sage
freshly ground black pepper
1 sheet ready-rolled puff pastry
1 egg, beaten

1 Preheat the oven to 180°C/350°F/gas mark 4.

2 Use your hands to blend the sausagemeat with the onion, sage and plenty of black pepper.

3 Cut 13 cm (5 in) wide strips of pastry and lay a generous mound of the sausage mixture along the length of the pastry.

4 Brush one edge with beaten egg, fold over the other and seal the two edges together with a fork. Cut into 5–8 cm (2–3 in) chunks and make two slits across the top of each one. Brush with the beaten egg, arrange on a dampened baking sheet and bake in the oven for 20–25 minutes.

Spiced chicken sandwiches

Use your favourite flavourings to create interesting sandwich spreads. This version mixes chicken with curry and chutney, and mayonnaise to keep the sandwiches moist.

SERVES 6

6 tbsp mayonnaise
3 tsp curry paste
2 tbsp mango chutney
12 slices good white sandwich bread
butter or margarine
4 cooked chicken breasts, sliced
1 crisp lettuce, shredded

1 Mix the mayonnaise, curry paste and chutney.

2 Spread the bread with the butter, then assemble the sandwiches.

Focaccia with rocket, Mozzarella and beef tomatoes

This is an ideal picnic sandwich as it's wrapped whole and you'll find the flavours have actually improved when you unpack it.

SERVES 6

1 focaccia
extra-virgin olive oil for drizzling
a handful of rocket leaves
200 g (7 oz) buffalo Mozzarella, shredded
2 beef tomatoes, sliced

1 Slice the focaccia horizontally into two rounds. (If it's thick, slice into three and use the middle section for croûtons.)

2 Drizzle the bottom round with olive oil, cover with rocket, Mozzarella and tomatoes and season well. Also drizzle the underside of the top piece of focaccia with olive oil before sandwiching the pieces together.

Clockwise from top left: smoked trout granary rolls with sage and onion sausage rolls, onion and potato frittata with mini pittas, spinach and feta and spiced chicken sandwiches, focaccia with rocket, Mozzarella and beef tomatoes.

Mini pittas with Mexican salad

The salad filling uses tinned beans to keep the recipe quick. Split the pittas and soften them in the microwave for a few seconds so they're easier to fill.

SERVES 6

300 g (11 oz) tin of mixed pulses, drained and rinsed
4 tbsp taco tomato sauce
6 mini pitta breads, split
1 oak leaf lettuce
150 g (5 oz) guacamole

1 Mix the pulses with the taco sauce.

2 Put them into the pitta breads with the lettuce and guacamole.

Smoked trout with horseradish and alfalfa on granary rolls

Tasty smoked trout fillets are readily available at fishmongers and at the wet fish counters in main supermarkets.

SERVES 6

3 tbsp creamed horseradish
2 tbsp mayonnaise
6 granary rolls
4 whole smoked trout fillets, boned
a small bag of alfalfa sprouts
salt and freshly ground black pepper

1 Mix the horseradish and mayonnaise and spread over the rolls.

2 Chop the trout into bite-sized pieces, add to the rolls and top with the alfalfa sprouts. Season well.

Easy hummus

This can be made up to three days in advance and stored in the fridge. Transport it to the picnic in a screw-topped jar and serve with an interesting selection of crudités.

SERVES 6

425 g (15 oz) tin of chick peas, drained and rinsed

1 large garlic clove

2 tbsp tahini paste

juice of 2 lemons

50 ml (2 fl oz) extra-virgin olive oil

salt and freshly ground black pepper

paprika

a few stoned black olives

1 Place the chick peas, garlic, tahini and lemon juice in a food processor and blend on full speed until the mixture forms a paste. On a low speed, gradually pour in the olive oil. If the mixture looks too dry, add a little warm boiled water to soften it.

2 Taste and season well with salt, pepper and more lemon juice if necessary. Serve sprinkled with a little paprika and garnished with black olives.

Spinach and Feta sandwiches with red peppers

You can substitute other small salad leaves for the spinach.

SERVES 6

2 red peppers

olive oil

a handful of baby spinach leaves

1 tbsp French dressing

250 g (9 oz) Feta cheese, sliced

12 slices wholemeal bread

butter or margarine

1 Drizzle the peppers with a little of the oil and grill for about 20 minutes until the skin is wrinkled and slightly charred. Place in a plastic bag and leave to cool.

2 Peel off and discard the skins and seeds. Thinly slice the flesh.

3 Toss the spinach with the French dressing.

4 Assemble the sandwiches with the peppers, spinach and Feta on the buttered bread.

Fruit kebabs with creamy meringue dip

This is easy to make – and to transport. Choose firm fruits that won't spoil on the kebab stick and try mixing them with ready-to-eat dried fruit, such as figs and apricots, to add texture. Once assembled, squeeze with lime juice so they won't discolour and finish with a wedge of lime to hold in place.

Crumble two meringues and a few drops of vanilla essence into 280 ml (9 fl oz) of double cream and store in a jar (keep well chilled using a wine cooler).

Really easy cheesy biscuits

These are perfect for serving with a variety of interesting cheeses. Avoid really high varieties if you are travelling any distance.

SERVES 6

100 g (4 oz) mature Cheddar cheese, diced

100 g (4 oz) butter, softened and diced

100 g (4 oz) plain flour

$\frac{1}{2}$ tsp salt

1 Preheat the oven to 180°C/350°F/gas mark 4.

2 Blend all the ingredients at high speed in a food processor until the mixture forms a ball. Don't overwork the mixture.

3 Roll out very thinly on a floured surface and cut into rounds. Bake in the oven on an ungreased baking tray for 20 minutes until pale golden brown.

The Great Beach Picnic

BRILLIANT PICNIC *treats on a seaside theme to appeal to both child and adult tastes. This selection is a classic combination of sweet and savoury flavours – along with a cooling drink to keep everyone refreshed.*

Mini tuna bites

These tasty little tuna fish cakes can be served either hot or cold.

MAKES 20

300 g (10 oz) potatoes, peeled and cubed

400 g (14 oz) tin of tuna chunks in brine, drained

10 spring onions, chopped

1 tbsp finely chopped fresh parsley

2 small eggs, beaten

a small pinch of cayenne pepper

salt and freshly ground black pepper

oil for frying

1 Boil the potatoes until soft, then mash until smooth and leave to cool.

2 Mix with the remaining ingredients except the oil and season. Form the mixture into 20 fish cakes.

3 Heat the oil in a heavy-based, non-stick frying pan and fry the fish cakes over a medium heat until crisp and golden.

4 Chill until ready to use, then serve with salsa or tomato ketchup.

Sausage seashells

This may sound a bit tricky, but you'll soon get the hang of it and the results are well worth the effort.

MAKES 16

4 giant skinless continental Frankfurters
275 g (10 oz) puff pastry
½ egg, beaten
2 tbsp sesame or poppy seeds

1 Preheat the oven to 220°C/425°F/gas mark 7.

2 Cut each Frankfurter into four pieces. Set aside. Cut the pastry in half. On a floured surface, roll each pastry piece into a 30 × 20 cm (12 × 18 in) rectangle. Straighten thre edges, then cut each rectangle into eight 30 cm (12 in) strips. For scalloped edges, use a pastry wheel.

3 To make the shells, brush one side of a pastry strip with water. Leaving about 2.5 cm (1 in) spare pastry at one end, wind the pastry strip round the sausage, water-brushed side facing the sausage, overlapping the edges of the pastry as you go. This will form the main shell and leave a spare piece of pastry at the other end of the sausage.

4 To form the top, twist the 2.5 cm (1 in) piece of spare pastry into a spiral shape. To form the bottom, press the spare pastry at the other end flat and curl up into a Catherine wheel.

5 Place the shells on a dampened non-stick baking sheet. Brush with the beaten egg and sprinkle with sesame or poppy seeds. Bake in the oven for about 20 minutes until golden brown and puffed up.

Clockwise from left: barbecued kebabs, mariners' pasties, individual salads served in orange halves and mini tuna bites.

Mariners' pasties

Tasty little pasties made with a vegetable and cheese filling, these are easy to transport and ideal picnic fare.

MAKES 12

1 tbsp corn oil
½ onion, very finely chopped
175 g (6 oz) new potatoes, scrubbed and diced
50 g (2 oz) carrots, diced
a pinch of dried thyme
1 tsp tomato purée
2 tbsp water
25 g (1 oz) mature Cheddar cheese, grated
salt and freshly ground black pepper
500 g (18 oz) shortcrust pastry
1 small egg, beaten with 1 tsp milk
1 tbsp black sesame seeds

1 Preheat the oven to 220°C/425°F/gas mark 7.

2 Heat the oil in a heavy-based frying pan and sauté the onion until soft and translucent.

3 Add the potatoes and carrots and cook briefly. Add the thyme, tomato purée and water. Cover and cook until the vegetables are tender. The mixture should be just moist. If necessary, remove the lid and cook briefly over high heat to reduce any excess liquid.

4 Remove from the heat and stir in the cheese and seasoning. Leave until cold.

5 Roll out the pastry and cut out 24 rounds.

6 Divide the filling between 12 of the rounds. Brush beaten egg or milk around the edge of each one and cover with the remaining pastry rounds. Press the edges firmly together with your fingers, brush with the egg wash and sprinkle the tops with the sesame seeds.

7 Bake in the oven for 15–20 minutes until golden.

Red and yellow pepper boats

Wrap these little boats in foil or clingfilm to transport.

SERVES 6

2 red peppers
2 yellow peppers
350 g (12 oz) cottage cheese
2 tbsp stoned green or black olives, chopped
2 tbsp cooked sweetcorn kernels
2 tbsp chopped celery
2 tbsp chopped cooked ham
1 tbsp snipped fresh chives

1 Cut peppers into segments along the lines running from the base to the top. Cut out the seeds to leave hollow sections.

2 Mix the cottage cheese with the olives, sweetcorn kernels, chopped celery and chopped ham.

3 Spoon into the pepper boats and sprinkle with chives.

Mermaid cakes

These cakes are similar to traditional fairy cakes but with the addition of raisins and a chocolate icing on top.

MAKES 16

120 g (4½ oz) soft margarine

75 g (3 oz) caster sugar

2 eggs, beaten

150 g (5 oz) plain flour

1 tsp baking powder

40 g (1½ oz) raisins, chopped

FOR THE TOPPING

200 g (7 oz) chocolate icing sugar, sifted

silver or coloured dragees

1 Preheat the oven to 200°C/400°F/gas mark 6. Line muffin trays with cases.

2 Cream the margarine and sugar. Gradually beat in the eggs. Sift together the flour and baking powder. Toss the chopped raisins in the flour mixture, then add to the batter, mixing well.

3 Half fill the paper cases with the batter. Bake in the oven for 10–15 minutes until golden brown and well risen. Leave to cool.

4 Place the icing sugar in a small bowl and mix in a little water a drop at a time until you have a smooth icing to spread over the cold cakes. Sprinkle with dragees, then leave the icing to set.

Fishy biscuits

Fishy in shape but not in flavour, our seaside biscuits are flavoured with orange. Writing icing is used to decorate the biscuits and is available from most supermarkets.

MAKES 30–35

225 g (8 oz) butter

1 egg, separated

50 g (2 oz) icing sugar, sifted

2 tbsp orange juice

450 g (1 lb) plain flour

coloured sugar strands

writing icing

1 Preheat the oven to 160°C/325°F/gas mark 3.

2 Cream the butter, egg yolk and sugar. Add the orange juice and flour. Work the dough quickly into a ball. Wrap in clingfilm and chill for 30 minutes.

3 Roll the dough out on a lightly floured surface to a thickness of about 1 cm (½ in) and make as many fish shapes as possible using a pastry cutter.

4 Arrange the cookies on non-stick baking sheets. Lightly beat the egg white, brush over the cookies, then sprinkle with sugar strands.

5 Bake in the oven for 20–25 minutes until lightly coloured. Allow to cool.

6 When the cookies have cooled completely, use the writing icing to outline tails, eyes and mouths on the fish.

Clockwise from top: double-decker jellies, chocolate sandcastles, fishy biscuits, mermaid cakes, melon thirst quencher.

Chocolate sandcastles

You'll need 100 g (4 oz) dariole moulds to make these moist little cakes. You can leave out the cocoa dusting if you're concerned about sticky fingers and faces!

MAKES 12

25 g (1 oz) butter, melted
600 ml (1 pint) milk
100 g (4 oz) plain chocolate, broken into pieces
50 g (2 oz) caster sugar
40 g (1½ oz) butter
165 g (5½ oz) fresh white breadcrumbs
2 eggs, beaten
1 tbsp cocoa powder

1 Preheat the oven to 160°C/325°F/gas mark 3. Brush the dariole moulds generously with the butter.

2 Place the milk, chocolate, sugar and butter in a heavy-based pan and heat gently, stirring, until the chocolate and butter have melted and the sugar has dissolved. Whisk until smooth.

3 Remove from the heat and stir in the breadcrumbs, then the eggs.

4 Divide the mixture between the moulds and bake in the oven for 40–45 minutes until a skewer inserted in the centre comes out clean. Turn out while still warm and dust with cocoa.

Double-decker jellies

If you wedge the glasses at alternate angles while the first two jelly flavours are setting, you can achieve an even more interesting and dramatic effect.

SERVES 6

600 ml (1 pint) banana juice
600 ml (1 pint) blackcurrant juice
600 ml (1 pint) apple juice
3 sachets of powdered gelatine
225 g (8 oz) blueberries

1 Pour the fruit juices into three separate bowls.

2 Dissolve the gelatine according to the packet instructions, adding one sachet to each bowl.

3 Divide the banana juice between plastic or acrylic glasses and chill until set. Keep the other juices at room temperature to stop them from setting.

4 For the second layer, scatter over two-thirds of the blueberries and pour over about half the blackcurrant juice. Allow to set, then add the rest of the blackcurrant mixture. Chill until set.

5 Finally, add the apple juice to each glass and chill until set. When set, top with the remaining blueberries.

Melon thirst quencher

This is a combined drink and dessert. Cut the top off a small watermelon and reserve the lid. Using a melon baller, scoop out as much of the melon as possible. Repeat with two different-coloured melons, such as honeydew and charantais, and add to the watermelon with black or green seedless grapes. Spoon into the empty melon shell, replace the lid and chill thoroughly.

BARBECUE EXTRAS
Disposable barbecues are perfect for the beach – just remember to anchor them firmly in the sand out of the wind, keep children away and make sure you put them out and dispose of them properly. Sausages and mixed vegetables on skewers are ideal, or try this simple chicken kebab recipe.

Cut chicken breast fillets into strips. Place between sheets of clingfilm and beat lightly with a rolling pin. Put the pieces into a large food bag and add a ready-made marinade. Thread the chicken on to metal skewers and transport in a cool box. Barbecue for about 5–6 minutes on each side.

The Movable Feast

ADULTS ENJOY *picnics as much as children but they want more sophisticated fare. So our hamper includes classic delights like lobster, asparagus and miniature summer puddings – all designed to be perfectly portable.*

Menu for six

TAPENADE WITH QUAILS' EGGS, ASPARAGUS AND CRUDITÉS

—

LOBSTERS IN THEIR SHELLS

SALAD ON STICKS

SOYA MAYONNAISE

WILD RICE SALAD

—

LITTLE INDIVIDUAL SUMMER PUDDINGS

—

WHITE WINE AND VODKA PUNCH

Tapenade with quails' eggs, asparagus and crudités

Provençal style tapenade starts the meal with a holiday flavour, and can be made several days in advance.

SERVES 6

2 x 50 g (2 oz) tins of anchovy fillets, drained, rinsed and chopped

100 g (4 oz) tinned tuna in oil, drained

225 g (8 oz) stoned black olives, roughly chopped

100 g (4 oz) capers in brine, drained

2 large garlic cloves, chopped

a few thyme leaves

2 tbsp brandy

200 ml (7 fl oz) extra virgin olive oil

a generous pinch of grated nutmeg

freshly ground black pepper

3 tbsp fresh white bread-crumbs

12–24 quails' eggs

350 g (12 oz) asparagus spears, trimmed

a selection of radishes, cherry tomatoes, tiny carrots and grissini sticks

1 Place the anchovy fillets, tuna, olives, capers, garlic, thyme and brandy in a food processor and process to a paste.

2 With the processor on medium speed, add the oil a few drops at a time, then in a slow, steady trickle, as when making mayonnaise, until all the oil is added.

3 Stir in the nutmeg and seasoning. Place in a screw-topped jar, cover and chill until ready to use.

4 Just before serving, stir in the breadcrumbs until well blended.

5 Boil the eggs for 2–3 minutes, then shell. Blanch the asparagus for 2 minutes, then drain.

6 Serve the tapenade with the eggs, asparagus and crudités with chunks of fresh, crusty bread.

Lobsters
in their shells

Buy ready-cooked lobsters from a good fishmonger. Once prepared, chill, and transport in a cool box to the picnic. To save time and effort, you can buy ready-prepared and dressed lobster halves from some good food shops and fishmongers. Crab is a delicious – and more economical – alternative to lobster, and can also be bought ready-prepared.

SERVES 6

3 x 675 g ($1\frac{1}{2}$ lb) cooked
   lobsters
6–9 tbsp mayonnaise
freshly ground black pepper
1 cos or other lettuce,
   shredded
flowerheads or large sprigs
   of dill to garnish

1 Work on one lobster at a time. First remove the claws by twisting them off. Crack the shell of the claws using a nutcracker or wooden mallet. Remove the flesh from the claws, taking care to discard all pieces of the shell. Place in a bowl and set aside.

2 Place the lobster, spine-uppermost, on a large chopping board. With the point of a large knife, pierce down through the cross at the centre of the head, then cut through the body and tail, dividing the body in half.

3 Turn the lobster over and cut through the head. Once the lobster is divided into two halves, remove the greenish liver (a delicacy) and the coral if the lobster is female, and add these to the bowl of claw meat.

4 Carefully discard the sac inside the head and the gills. Remove and discard the intestinal vein which runs along the lobster's tail. All the remaining parts of the lobster are edible.

5 Lift out the flesh from the lobster tails in one piece and lay it curved-side upwards on a chopping board. Slice it into bite-sized pieces.

6 Put the cut lobster meat back into the shells, reversing it so that the curved side is uppermost – this looks prettier and more colourful.

7 Roughly chop the reserved flesh from the claws and bind with a little mayonnaise. Season with black pepper and mix with the liver and coral.

8 Line the lobster head with a little shredded lettuce, then divide the mixture between the heads of the lobster halves.

Dressed lobster is a delicious treat for a grown-up picnic and the shells provide their own serving dishes.

9 Wrap the prepared lobster halves in clingfilm and chill. Repeat with the remaining lobsters.

Salad on sticks

By far the easiest way to serve picnic salads is to thread crisp salad leaves or small lettuce wedges on to wooden skewers, interspersed with cucumber batons and strips of pepper, brushed with a little olive oil mixed with crushed garlic. Place on a serving platter, cover with clingfilm and chill. Serve with a vinaigrette dressing.

Soya mayonnaise

This recipe makes about 350 ml (12 fl oz) and will keep for a couple of weeks in a screw-topped jar in the fridge. For best results when making mayonnaise, all the ingredients should be at room temperature.

SERVES 6

2 egg yolks
a pinch of cayenne pepper
a pinch of ground white pepper
2 tbsp lemon juice or tarragon vinegar
2 tsp soy sauce
300 ml (10 fl oz) sunflower or grapeseed oil
½ small garlic clove, crushed

1 Place the egg yolks, cayenne and white pepper, lemon juice or vinegar and soy sauce in a food processor. Blend on high until the mixture is pale and creamy.

2 Place the oil in a jug. With the processor on high speed, start adding the oil a drop at a time until about one-third of the oil has been added. Add the remaining oil in a slow, steady stream.

3 Stir in the garlic and spoon into a screw-topped jar. Store in the fridge.

Wild rice salad

If possible use mixed packets of wild and long-grain rice. If you buy them separately, check the cooking times before you mix them as wild rice may take longer to cook.

SERVES 6

- 175 g (6 oz) wild and long-grain rice, mixed
- 2 tsp clear honey
- 2 tsp wholegrain mustard
- 4 tsp soy sauce
- 4 tsp lemon juice
- 4 tsp olive oil
- 1 tbsp sunflower oil
- 250 g (9 oz) oyster mushrooms, torn into thin strips
- 6 spring onions, thinly sliced
- 2 tbsp chopped fresh coriander (optional)

1 Cook the rice in lightly salted water according to the packet instructions.

2 Blend the honey, mustard, soy sauce, lemon juice and olive oil.

3 Heat the sunflower oil in a heavy non-stick pan and cook the mushroom strips over a high heat until golden brown. Remove from the heat and leave to cool.

4 Drain the cooked rice and rinse in cold water. Toss the rice and mushrooms into the dressing. Stir in the onions and coriander, if using.

Little individual summer puddings

These individual versions of the classic recipe are irresistible. Use small foil or plastic pudding basins or tea cups which will hold about 250 ml (9 fl oz).

SERVES 6

- 450 g (1 lb) raspberries
- 225 g (8 oz) redcurrants
- 175 g (6 oz) blackberries
- 150–175 g (5–6 oz) caster sugar
- 4 tbsp water
- 24 slices medium-cut white or wholemeal bread from a small loaf, crusts removed
- a few bunches of redcurrants
- 300 ml (10 fl oz) crème fraîche or pouring cream

1 Place the fruits, sugar and water in a pan. Cover and simmer gently for about 5 minutes until the fruit is just soft.

Opposite: *Lobster served with wild rice salad, asparagus and salad on sticks.*

2 Cut six circular pieces of bread to cover the bottom of the basins. Then cut the remaining bread to fit the sides of the basins, allowing the edges to overlap a little.

3 Brush the prepared bread with a little of the fruit juice, then press firmly into the basins to line, making sure there are no gaps between the pieces of bread.

4 Divide the fruit between the lined basins. Cut the remaining bread to cover the filled basins.

5 Cover with clingfilm and place a weight on top. Place the puddings on a dish to catch the juices. Chill overnight.

6 To serve, invert on to individual plates. Decorate with redcurrants and serve with crème fraîche or cream.

White wine and vodka punch

A refreshing drink with the sharp tang of limes, this slips down easily but still packs quite a 'punch'.

SERVES 6–8

- 4 bottles dry white wine
- ½ bottle vodka
- 200 ml (7 fl oz) tonic water
- 2 limes, sliced
- ice cubes
- mint sprigs

1 Mix the wine, vodka and tonic water. Add the sliced limes and chill well.

2 Pour into a jug and add ice cubes and mint sprigs to serve.

The Barbecue Dinner Party

*E*NJOY THE *real luxury of alfresco eating with a classic dinner party that can be cooked entirely in the open. This menu lets you barbecue everything from the prawn starter to the baby potatoes — leaving just the pudding to bake gently while you're eating.*

Smoked meats and melon salad

Smoked, sliced venison and chicken are available from delicatessens and some supermarkets. If you prefer, you can use Parma ham, bresaola, salami, smoked sliced turkey or ham instead.

SERVES 6

1 large radicchio, shredded
75–100 g (3–4 oz) rocket
  leaves
1 small ripe melon, halved,
  seeded and chilled
100 g (4 oz) smoked
  venison, sliced
250 g (9 oz) smoked
  chicken, skinned and
  sliced
3 tbsp olive or walnut oil
1 tbsp balsamic vinegar
a pinch of sugar
salt and freshly ground
  black pepper

1 Arrange the shredded radicchio and rocket leaves on a large serving plate. Cut each melon half into three wedges. Peel the wedges and fan out on the plate, laying the smoked meat on top of the melon.

2 Blend the oil, vinegar and sugar to make the dressing and spoon over the salad, melon and meats. Season with black pepper and serve with hot bread.

3 If prepared some time in advance, arrange the salad, cover with clingfilm and chill until ready to serve. Dress the salad just before serving.

Barbecued Halloumi cheese

Halloumi is a semi-hard Greek cheese, usually made from ewe's milk, which is sold in 350 g (12 oz) blocks. The texture is quite chewy and the flavour is salty. When barbecued, it makes a great first course. Hinged wire racks for grilling are available from barbecue retailers.

SERVES 6

350 g (12 oz) Halloumi cheese
olive oil
freshly ground black pepper

1 Rinse the cheese thoroughly in lots of cold water to remove excess salt. Dry well on kitchen paper and cut into 5 mm ($\frac{1}{4}$ in) slices.

2 Place the sliced cheese in hinged wire racks, Brush the slices generously with olive oil and season with pepper. Grill over a medium heat for about 1 minute on each side or until the cheese is speckled brown. Serve at once as the cheese becomes tough and rubbery when cold.

Spicy barbecued prawns

Ready-made black bean sauce straight from the bottle gives a delicious flavour to barbecued prawns. The prawns will need peeling before eating, so provide lots of paper napkins and perhaps some finger bowls of tepid water with slices of lemon for your guests to rinse their hands.

SERVES 6

18–24 large raw tiger prawns
160 g (5$\frac{1}{2}$ oz) bottle of stir-fry black bean sauce
1 lemon or 1–2 limes, cut into wedges

1 Remove and discard the heads from the prawns by twisting them off. Wash the prawns thoroughly and dry on kitchen paper. Place in a shallow dish, pour over the black bean sauce and toss well. Cover and set aside for at least 30 minutes.

2 Thread the prawns on to skewers, three to four prawns per skewer, and barbecue over a medium heat for 2–3 minutes on each side until the prawns turn pink and are cooked through. Be careful not to overcook the prawns or the flesh will begin to toughen.

3 Serve with lemon or lime wedges.

QUICK BARBECUE TIPS
Allow enough time for the charcoal to heat up. It's ready when the ashes are gently glowing, but it's vital to wait until the flames die down before you start cooking. Charcoal barbecues give food a smoky flavour, but if you have a gas barbecue, you can spice up your food by sprinkling aromatic woodchips on the lava rock. Make sure the barbecue isn't set up in an area exposed to the wind. Keep turning the food so that it cooks evenly. Serve food immediately, or place at the edge of the grill so that it stays hot.

Clockwise from top: smoked meats and melon salad, barbecued Halloumi cheese, spicy barbecued prawns, served with a crusty ciabatta loaf.

Grilled salmon teriyaki-style

Fish is perfect for marinating because the marinade flavours are absorbed very quickly. Oily fish such as salmon barbecues especially well.

SERVES 6

6 x 150–175 g (5–6 oz) salmon steaks

FOR THE TERIYAKI SAUCE

120 ml (4 fl oz) Japanese soy sauce

120 ml (4 fl oz) dry sherry

120 ml (4 fl oz) balsamic vinegar

40 g (1½ oz) caster sugar

a pinch of crushed dried chilli peppers

juice of ½ lemon

1 tsp fresh thyme leaves

TO FINISH

3–4 tbsp sunflower oil

salt and freshly ground black pepper

1 lemon or 1–2 limes, cut into wedges

1 bunch of spring onions, halved lengthways

1 Wipe the fish on kitchen paper and place in a single layer in a shallow dish.

2 Blend the marinade ingredients and pour over the fish. Cover and leave for 30–60 minutes, turning the fish over once.

3 When ready to cook, place the fish steaks inside oiled hinged wire racks. Brush the fish with oil and season with a little salt and pepper, bearing in mind that the marinade is quite salty.

4 Barbecue the salmon over a medium heat for 3–4 minutes on each side, brushing with marinade or oil as required. The fish is ready when the flesh flakes when tested with a fork.

5 Arrange the spring onions on a large plate, place the fish on top and garnish with lemon or lime wedges.

Golden grilled new potatoes

1 Scrub small, even-sized potatoes well and boil in salted water for 10 minutes. Drain and toss in a little olive oil. Season with salt and freshly ground black pepper.

2 Place the potatoes in hinged wire racks with sprigs of rosemary, if desired. Barbecue for 10–15 minutes or until golden brown, turning the broiler over from time to time and brushing the potatoes with oil as required.

Mixed barbecued vegetables

The cooking time for the different vegetables varies considerably, so it's best to barbecue each type separately, either threaded on to skewers or in hinged wire racks.

Clockwise from right: golden grilled new potatoes and mixed barbecued vegetables, grilled salmon teriyaki-style, served with a crisp green salad.

Red onion kebabs

Medium-sized red onions are best for this recipe, although ordinary onions will do.

1 Peel and halve the onions, then cut each half into three wedges.

2 Thread the wedges on to skewers, brush with oil and season with salt and freshly ground black pepper.

3 Barbecue the onions for about 20 minutes, turning the skewers over frequently and brushing with oil as required, until they are nicely browned and thoroughly cooked.

Green and yellow courgette kebabs

1 Wash and trim green and yellow courgettes and cut then into 4 cm (1½ in) lengths.

2 Thread the courgette pieces on to skewers. Crush a garlic clove into a little oil and brush over the vegetables.

3 Season with salt and freshly ground black pepper. Barbecue for about 15 minutes, turning the skewers over every so often and brushing with oil as required, until the courgettes are cooked through and golden brown.

Summer cherry clafoutis

This dessert is a French summer classic, and is quick and easy to make. A slightly acidic cherry is best, although most other types are fine.
Remember to give yourself time to stone the cherries.

SERVES 6

25 g (1 oz) unsalted butter
700 g (1½ lb) cherries, stalks and stones removed
3 large eggs
1 egg yolk
50–75 g (2–3 oz) caster sugar
40 g (1½ oz) plain flour
450 ml (15 fl oz) milk
200 ml (7 fl oz) single cream
3 tbsp brandy or Kirsch
icing sugar, sifted
single cream or crème fraîche

1 Grease a gratin dish large enough to hold the cherries in one layer in the bottom of the dish.

2 Beat together the eggs, egg yolk, sugar, flour, milk and cream. Strain the batter over the fruit and set aside for 30 minutes.

3 Preheat the oven to 200°C/400°F/gas mark 6.

4 Bake in the oven for 35–40 minutes or until the custard is puffed up and golden brown.

5 Drizzle the brandy or Kirsch over the pudding and lightly dust with the icing sugar. Serve warm with single cream or crème fraîche, as preferred.

Index